MOONS[

Snoo Wilson

Methuen

Published by Methuen 1999

1 3 5 7 9 10 8 6 4 2

First published in the United Kingdom by
Methuen Publishing Limited
215 Vauxhall Bridge Road
London SW1V 1EJ

Peribo Pty Ltd, 58 Beaumont Road, Mount Kuring-Gai,
NSW 2080, Australia, ACN 002 273 761
(for Australia and New Zealand)

Methuen Publishing Limited Reg. No. 3543167

A CIP catalogue record is available from the British Library

ISBN 0 413 74510 4

Typeset by SX Composing DTP, Rayleigh, Essex
Printed and bound in Great Britain by
Cox & Wyman Ltd, Reading, Berkshire

Hampstead Theatre and the Theatre Royal Plymouth
present the world premiere of

MOONSHINE
by Snoo Wilson

Cast in order of appearance

Sir Arthur Conan Doyle	Robin Soans
Weegee	Pui Fan Lee
Abraxas	Ian Gelder
Serena	Ingeborga Dapkunaite
Arsile	Sarah Cartwright
Morgue	Lisa Ellis
Moloch	Peter Jonfield

Director	Simon Stokes
Designer	Robin Don
Costume Designer	Maria Ahnhem
Lighting	Giuseppe Di Iorio
Sound	Mike Palmer

Moonshine was originally commissioned by Hampstead Theatre,
Artistic Director Jenny Topper.

Hampstead Theatre is a registered charity - No. 218506

 FUNDED BY CAMDEN COUNCIL

Theatre Royal Plymouth Ltd is a registered charity - No. 284545

Supported by Cornwall County Council
Supported by Devon County Council

Smart people in search of adventure.....

...is how the 50,000 people who attend Hampstead Theatre each year have been described. The adventure they're on is the discovery of new plays by both undiscovered and prestigious playwrights, exciting acting talent and high quality productions. Our business is producing new and contemporary plays to the highest possible standards and we are able to do so by working with a formidable assembly of talented directors, designers and actors - a fraction of whom are listed below.....

Jane Asher   Kate Ashfield   Frances Barber   Helen Baxendale   Jim Broadbent
Niall Buggy   John Byrne   Anthony Calf   Peter Capaldi   Martin Clunes
George Cole   Tom Conti   Niamh Cusack   Sorcha Cusack   Lindsay Duncan
Faye Dunaway   Rupert Everett   Adam Faith   Albert Finney   Brad Fraser
Michael Frayn   Maria Friedman   Brian Friel   David Haig   Jonathan Harvey
Jane Horrocks   Geraldine James   Paul Jesson   Alex Kingston   Tony Kushner
Belinda Lang   Larry Lamb   Jude Law   Denis Lawson   Mike Leigh
Maureen Lipman   Phyllis Logan   John Malkovich   Miriam Margolyes
Alec McCowan   Ewan McGregor   Tim McInnerny   Kevin McNally
Rona Munro   Julia Ormond   Michael Pennington   Alan Plater
Stephen Poliakoff   Stephen Rea   Corin Redgrave   Saskia Reeves
Alan Rickman   Philip Ridley   Tim Roth   Rufus Sewell   David Schneider
Dougray Scott   Anthony Sher   Mel Smith   Imelda Staunton   Alison Steadman
Shelagh Stephenson   David Suchet   Gwen Taylor   Harriet Walter
Julie Walters   Zoe Wanamaker   Timberlake Wertenbaker   Greg Wise   John Wood

A theatrical powerhouse and much more...

"At what other serious theatre can you drop in for a do-it-yourself cup of tea and natter? And where do cast and audience booze more comfortably together after the show? Nowhere is á happy full house more gratifying than at Hampstead" Mike Leigh

By becoming a member of Hampstead Theatre you will receive advance information on Hampstead Theatre productions, in the West End and on tour, as well as discounts on tickets. Contact the Box Office on 020 7722 9301.

Hampstead Theatre, Swiss Cottage Centre, 98 Avenue Road, London NW3 3EX

Artistic Director	Jenny Topper
General Manager	James Williams
Literary Manager	Ben Jancovich
Associate Directors	Gemma Bodinetz
	Jonathan Church
	John Dove
	Robin Lefèvre

The Theatre Royal Plymouth, opened in 1982, has become one of the largest and best attended regional producing theatres in Britain and the leading promoter of theatre in the South West. An ever-expanding range of activity has, in recent years, seen the Theatre achieve popular success, critical acclaim and artistic excellence, with annual audiences of over 400,000.

As well as welcoming the leading touring drama, opera and dance companies to the South West, the Theatre Royal produces or co-produces a number of new drama and musical productions each year, many of which go on to find audiences elsewhere, either on tour or in London.

PREMIERES

Recent premieres have included: *The Impostor* by Pete Lawson (based on Moliere's Tartuffe); *A Time And A Season* by Alex Shearer; *A Soldier's Song* by Hugh Janes; *The King Of Prussia* by Nick Darke (with Kneehigh Theatre) and *China Song* (with Clear Day Productions). European premieres have included *Tiger Tail* by Tennessee Williams and an adaptation of William Wharton's *Birdy*, which went on to be presented at the Lyric Theatre, Hammersmith and Comedy Theatre, London.

In September 1998 the Theatre Royal produced the European premiere of the New York hit *Gross Indecency: The Three Trials Of Oscar Wilde*, which completed a run at the Gielgud Theatre on Shaftesbury Avenue.

THE ROYAL SHAKESPEARE COMPANY

More than 40,000 tickets were sold for each of the Royal Shakespeare Company's Plymouth seasons in 1997 and 1998. Over a period of four weeks the full Stratford-Upon-Avon repertoire was presented in the Theatre Royal, Drum Theatre (the Theatre Royal's studio theatre) and a specially built auditorium in Plymouth Pavilions. The RSC will return to Plymouth for a third season in spring 2000.

BEYOND THE SOUTH WEST

1996 saw six Theatre Royal productions running concurrently in the West End - *Buddy*, *Jolson, Fame, Passion, Tolstoy* and *Birdy* - and acclaim for Laurence Boswell's production of *Long Day's Journey Into Night*.

Other recent successes include *West Side Story*, a co-production with Pola Jones and currently at the Prince Of Wales Theatre and a new production of *Hamlet* with the Young Vic, which was also seen in Japan in July 1999. The Theatre Royal's relationship with Cameron Mackintosh has resulted in the launch of *Les Miserables* and *The Phantom Of The Opera* national tours and a co-production of the national tour of *Oliver!*. Co-productions that open in London this autumn include *Great Balls Of Fire: The Jerry Lee Lewis Story, Spend, Spend, Spend* and *Hedda Gabler*.

EDUCATION

The Theatre Royal's Education Team provides an essential resource for developing audiences. It runs the largest youth theatre in Britain (The Young Company) and the community theatre (The People's Company). Young Company successes include the music theatre production of *Korczak*, which was seen in Plymouth, London and Poland.

Chief Executive	Adrian Vinken
Artistic Director	Simon Stokes
Associate Directors	Laurence Boswell
	Jennie Darnell
	Nick Stimson

An introduction by Snoo Wilson

This play is firstly intended to intrigue the audience into following an invented story about the thoroughly decent and honourable Arthur Conan Doyle's relationship with Sherlock Holmes, after he had killed off the great detective. The modern spirit discounts the idea of entities incorporated into the material world. In the days of the ancients they were comfortable with co-existence and used it to describe the workings of fate. Doyle, a believer, was mocked for his belief in spiritualism and modern fairies. Nowadays it is all so different.

Quantum physics upsets notions of probability and indeed appears to make a mockery of many ideas of the here-and-now. For instance, it has been for a while a quite respectable hypothesis that the universe (or everything) is in its present form because it is a 'mistake', being a mis-accounting between matter and antimatter. Shortly, it seems, more accurate Universe-style accountancy could be in place, the result being that we ludicrous beasts of the space-time continuum will disappear like quarks in the night, and things will be non-existent again. I'm not sure what I think about all this, because I am not a physicist, but we are only just venturing outside the nursery door and things will continue to get more amazing: which is, of course, where theatre comes into its own.

Abraxas 365's name corresponds to an invocation of the godhead used by the first and second century Christian gnostics, who proclaimed a duality of matter and spirit. Abraxas is also the name given to one of Aurora's horses. Since Aurora's function was to bring on the dawn, I have assumed for the purpose of the play that Abaraxas 365 was among the first monotheistic totems of Iran. I have made him a pre-Zoroastrian sun-god dwelling far above the mess of the material world, whose one fleeting moment of self-doubt had given rise to The Adversary, the devil, Moloch, or what you will.

Moloch, or Molech or Milcom, was a god of human sacrifice. In the middle east around this time he certainly eclipsed Jarweh for a while. Abraham was following tradition, when he was instructed from On High to follow Jarweh's instruction to sacrifice a ram rather than his son.

This suggests a reason why Judaism may have prospered at its bloodier rival's expense. At the end of the day, the Molochites may have sacrificed themselves into oblivion. The doctrine of survival of the fittest, as applied to competitive religions, appears to work perfectly well although Darwinian casuality bends to the belief that the future is always unknowable. However, with enough supergravity strings under one's belt, it is theoretically possible that time travel can happen. It is strange that the quark-and-meson universe might provide ammunition to demolish the framework in which Darwin's ideas operate, but it is not unthinkable.

A few months ago I chiselled out a preface to affix to my first volume of

Methuen collected plays. Looking at what I wrote so chestily, I realise that in common with the plays, the credo probably 'plays' out loud better than it reads on the page. This to my sorrow, has been a constant comment on the play over the years. It was fashionable before St Augustine to read everything out loud. In order to steep themselves in understanding, no self respecting reader kept things to himself, but now with the voice 'on the page' moving inside, to the imagination, sometimes things get lost.

What you hold in your hand is a cleaned-up version of what the Elizabethans called Fowle Papers: the clean up continues. Even being a Modern Person and having a word processor, I accumulated enough Fowle Papers in this play to provide nests for any number of hens. I should like to thank Jenny Topper of Hampstead Theatre, who commissioned the play, and the director Simon Stokes of the Theatre Royal Plymouth, for dealing with these farmyard matters with tact and sympathy. All the faults are mine, but if the play delights anyone's mind and imagination, then the glory reflects on my editors, Simon and Jenny, too.

Snoo Wilson

Snoo's writing has been described as "a fantastic toyshop whose timeless contraptions - genuine luxury goods from all the ages - whirr, fizz and explode in their collisions as if by magic". He is a distinguished playwright with a long list of plays to his name, including: *Vampire*; *Pignight*; an adaptation of Venedict Erofyev's *Walpurgis Night* for The Gate; *The Number Of The Beast*, *More Light* and *Darwin's Flood* (directed by Simon Stokes) and most recently *Sabina* all for The Bush and *HRH*, first performed at Theatr Clwyd and revived last Autumn for a No 1 Tour, followed by a run at the Playhouse Theatre starring Amanda Donohoe as Wallis Simpson and Corin Redgrave as Edward Windsor. *HRH* is the recent recipient of the Eileen Anderson/Central Broadcasting Premiere Award for Best Night Out. Snoo's work has been produced by the Royal Shakespeare Company, the Royal Court and throughout the United States. He has written films, librettos and radio plays - including two scripts about Dr Johnson, played by Simon Callow, for the BBC. Libretti include: an acclaimed adaptation of Offenbach's *Orpheus In The Underworld* for the English National Opera at the Coliseum and recently produced by Holland Park Opera; the book for *80 Days* at the La Jolla Playhouse in California and *The Bedbug*, with musicians Guy Pratt and Gary Kemp, originally commissioned as a play by the Royal National Theatre. Snoo's novel *I, Crowley* is published by Mandrake, and Methuen are currently publishing the first two volumes of Collected Works.

Future projects include a film of *Sabina*, scheduled to start shooting in 2000, starring Paul McGann.

Sarah Cartwright - Arsile

Sarah recently graduated from the Italia Conti Academy.

Theatre credits include: *War Dance*; *Dermott*; *Boyfriend From Hell*; *East*; *Snap!* and *Knife Games*.

Television: *Nightclub*; *Silent Witness* and *London's Burning*.

Film: *Bedside Mountaineers* and *Going Straight*.

Ingeborga Dapkunaite - Serena

Theatre credits include: *After Darwin* (Hampstead Theatre); *Libra* (Steppenwolf Theatre, Chicago); *A Slip Of The Tongue* (Steppenwolf Theatre & West End) and extensive work in Lithuania, where she won the Best Actress Award in 1992.

Television: *Sex And Death*; *Big Bad World*; *The Professionals*; *Thieftakers* and *On Dangerous Ground*.

Recent films include: *Shadow Of The Vampire*; *Seven Years In Tibet*; *Mission Impossible*; *Burnt By The Sun* (Academy Award for Best Foreign Film & Grand Prix de Jury - Cannes Film Festival); *Katia Ismailova* (Best Actress - Russian Film Academy Awards & Best Actress Special Jury Prize - Geneva Film Festival) and *Cynics* (Best Newcomer - Critics Circle Award, Russia).

Lisa Ellis - Morgue

Lisa graduated from Central School of Speech and Drama in 1998.

Theatre credits include: *Trips* (Birmingham Rep) and *Popcorn* (West End).

Television: *Holby City II*; *Devices And Desires* and *The Story Teller*.

Film: *Gangster No.1* and *Simple Things*.

Radio: *Little Angels*.

Ian Gelder - Abraxas

Theatre credits include: *Apocalyptica* and *Marvin's Room* (Hampstead Theatre); *Poor Superman* (Hampstead Theatre & Traverse Theatre); *Good* and *The Front Page* (Donmar); *Martin Yesterday* (Manchester Royal Exchange); *Anna Karenina* (Shared Experience); *Huckleberry Finn* and *Entertaining Mr Sloane* (Greenwich Theatre); *Mrs Warren's Profession* (Lyric, Hammersmith) and *Two Lips Indifferent Red* (Bush).

Television: *McCallum*; *Casualty*; *Absolutely Fabulous*; *Chandler & Co*; *Poirot*; *Ruth Rendell* and *The Day Today*.

Film: *King Ralph* and *Jinnah*.

Peter Jonfield - Moloch

Theatre credits include: *Four Door Saloon* and *The Water Engine* (Hampstead Theatre); *Shang-A-Lang* (Bush); *Loot* (Theatre Royal Plymouth); *Plunder* (West End & tour); *The Government Inspector* (Greenwich Theatre) and *Scenes From An Execution* (Almeida Theatre).

Most recent television includes: *Heartbeat*; *Badger*; *Silent Witness*; *The Bill*; *Smith & Jones*; *Noah's Ark*; *The Famous Five Series II* and *Bramwell*.

Films include: *Mary Shelley's Frankenstein*; *McVicar*; *Let Him Have It* and *A Fish Called Wanda*.

Pui Fan Lee - Weegee

Theatre credits include: *The Baby* (Bush); *Cinderella*, *Jack And The Beanstalk*, *Ali Baba* and *Red Riding Hood* (London Bubble); *The Lower Depths* (Cardboard Citizens) and her one woman show *Short, Fat, Ugly & Chinese*.

Television: *Teletubbies*; *Chef!*; *Frank Stubbs II*; *Murphy's Mob*; *Your Mother Wouldn't Like It*, *Josephine Jo*; *The Bill* and *Desmonds*.

Film: *The Big Push* and *The Worst Witch*.

Radio: *The Fitting*; *Kai Mei Sauce*; *The Moon Lady*; *Short, Fat, Ugly & Chinese* and *Better Left Unsaid*.

Robin Soans
- Sir Arthur Conan Doyle

Theatre credits include: *The Positive Hour* (Hampstead Theatre/Out of Joint); *Hamlet* (Young Vic); *The London Cuckolds, The Invention Of Love* and *Volpone* (RNT); *Shopping And Fucking* (Royal Court/Out of Joint); *Waiting Room Germany, Star-Gazie Pie & Sauerkraut* and *Three Birds Alighting On A Field* (Royal Court) and *The Country Wife, Venetian Twins* and *Murder In The Cathedral* (RSC).

Television: *Inspector Morse*; *Kavanagh QC*; *Far From The Madding Crowd*; *Jonathon Creek* and *Rebecca*.

Film: *Sabotage*; *Comrades* and *Blue Juice*.

Simon Stokes - Director

Simon Stokes was an Artistic Director at the Bush Theatre from the mid-70's to the late 80's. Thereafter, alongside a freelance career, he was an Artistic Associate and Director of Development for the Turnstyle Group in London's West End until the mid-90's. He is currently the Artistic Director at the Theatre Royal, Plymouth.

A new play specialist, he developed and directed many of our now established playwrights, along with a generation of now leading actors. Trained at the Bristol Old Vic Theatre School, he has directed in Germany, Switzerland, Israel and the U.S.A, as well as in Great Britain.

His most highly profiled work has included West End successes - *When I Was A Girl I Used To Scream And Shout* by Sherman Macdonald (with Julie Walters, Geraldine James and Dawn French) at the Whitehall Theatre and *A Slip Of The Tongue* by Dusty Hughes (with John Malkovich and Ingeborga Dapkunaite) at the Shaftesbury Theatre.

As an occasional actor, he has played Edward in Richard Eyre's film *The Ploughman's Lunch*, scripted by Ian McEwan, opposite Jonathan Pryce and Tim Curry, and is beaten up by Jennifer Saunders as Saffy's lecherous lecturer, Gerald, in the penultimate episode of *Absolutely Fabulous*.

He often produced Snoo Wilson plays at the Bush Theatre and directed the successful productions of *More Light* and *Darwin's Flood* there, both with Robin Don as designer.

Robin Don - Designer

Theatre credits include: *Someone Who'll Watch Over Me* (Hampstead Theatre, Vaudeville & Broadway); *The Rocky Horror Show* (currently on tour); *A Long Day's Journey Into Night* (Gate Theatre, Dublin); *The Storm* (Almeida); *Of Mice And Men* (West Yorkshire Playhouse); *Steaming* (Piccadilly Theatre); *The Shallow End* (Royal Court); *Fool For Love* (Donmar); Picasso's *Four Little Girls, Sherlock's Last Case* and *Anatol* (Open Space); *When I Was A Girl I Used To Scream And Shout* (Whitehall, Bush and Edinburgh Festival); *Kiss Of The*

Spiderwoman, *The Marshalling Yard*, *More Light* and *Darwin's Flood* (Bush Theatre); *Beautiful Thing* (Bush, Donmar & West End); *The Ticket Of Leave Man* (RNT); *Twelfth Night* and *Les Enfants Du Paradis* (RSC); *A Walk In The Woods* (Comedy Theatre) and *Song And Dance* (Palace Theatre).

Opera and Ballet designs include productions for: Opera de Lyon; San Francisco Opera; Royal Opera House, Covent Garden; Australian Opera and Santiago de Chile Ballet.

In 1996 the Critics Circle awarded him Designer of the Year for the production of *The Winter Guest* at the Almeida Theatre. He was production designer of the film *The Winter Guest,* which premiered at the 1997 Venice Film Festival and he has now succumbed to this!

Maria Ahnhem - Costume Designer

Trained at Wimbledon School of Art.

Set and costume designs include: *Celaine* and *No Exp. Req'd.* (Hampstead Theatre); *Kickin* and *Closed Circuit* both by Gerry Nowicki for the Wimbledon Studio Theatre; *The Cat Journey*, a childrens production for a Swedish tour; Tjechov's *The Bear* and Lady Gregory's *When The Moon Rises* for the Osteraker Ensemble in Sweden.

Maria has recently designed a London showcase of St George And The Dragon.

Giuseppe Di Iorio - Lighting

Giuseppe has worked extensively in the theatre in the UK since 1992 after training at the Guildhall School of Music and Drama.

Recent theatre work includes: *A Midsummer Night's Dream* (National Youth Theatre) and *The Moment Is A Gift, That's Why They Call It The Present* (produced by Paines Plough and performed during the 1999 Miu Miu/Prada Fashion Show in Milan). Also, *El Quijote* (Gate Theatre); *Happy and Glorious* by Richard Vincent (Warehouse, Croydon) and *Ai Carmela* (Riverside). Giuseppe co-founded the Hourglass Theatre Company which have performed in Italy and the UK - their most recent production being *Marathon* in Paris.

Recent lighting designs for Opera include: *Hugh The Drover* and *Macbeth* (English Touring Opera); *Broken Strings* and *Snatched By The Gods* by Param Vir (Scottish Opera); *A Midsummer Night's Dream* (1998 Aldeburgh Festival); *Boris Godunov* for the Kirov (Drury Lane) and *The Country Of The Blind* (English National Opera Contemporary Opera Studio - currently exhibited at the Theatre Museum).

Dance includes *Dances With Death* (Royal Ballet) and *Percussive Feet* (Dance Umbrella).

Giuseppe is shortly to light *Sankofa* by Adzido, and *Rinaldo* for the Guildhall School of Music and, next year *The Marriage Of Figaro* for Opera Theatre Company, Dublin.

He is a Theatre Design course lecturer at St Martins.

Moonshine

Characters

Sir Arthur Conan Doyle
Abraxas, Lord of Heaven
Serena, Queen of Heaven
Moloch, *a magnate, son of Abraxas*
Morgue
Arsile } *twin daughters of Moloch*
Weegee, *assistant to Doyle and Moloch*

Act One

*Two cloaked figures, struggling to strangle each other, against a
backdrop of crashing water, lit by lightning flashes.*

Doyle *enters, perhaps from the audience, a dominating, squarish
Edwardian with a walrus moustache. The noise of water fades, the
lights on the figures go out.*

Doyle   What would you say, ladies and gentlemen, to the
perpetrator of a coolly premeditated murder, when he
shamelessly introduced himself to you? What would your
reaction be if the killer appeared to show no regret for his
act, indeed boasted of his crime to law-abiding citizens, like
you? Just such a murderous ruffian stands before you. The
death of my victim, far from arousing feelings of remorse in
me, was experienced as an upsurge, a profound personal
release, at first.

Writing to my dear mother of my lethal intentions, I told
her that I was going to arrange for Sherlock Holmes' fatal
tumble over the Richenbach Falls with Moriarty and,
furthermore, I was looking forward to getting rid of him.
Motive? I was tired of standing in the shadow of my
creation, and I had many other books in me. Lost worlds
and the age of chivalry were all infinitely more rewarding to
produce than the Great Detective's elephantine deductions,
which I was creating less and less rejoicingly.

I now raise, if not the curtain, then something very like it,
on a chilling personal drama, the story of how a writer came
to be haunted by the ghost of his own former creation.

*Lights on the struggle again. Two figures commence trying to strangle
each other, again. Then* **Abraxas** *and* **Serena** *are discovered.*
Serena*'s dress is vast and floral;* **Abraxas** *is concealed for the
moment in the foliage train blurring into Cottingley.*

Doyle   Shortly after the end of the First World War, I had
proposed to a committee for the Great London Spiritualist

Association a follow-up vigil to be conducted in Yorkshire to record the controversial Cottingley fairies a second time, if possible, on camera. The first evidence had been obtained by two innocent young girls from a rural working-class Yorkshire family, using their father's box-camera. The fairies recorded were of human shape, not more than an inch or so high, with gossamer wings. To my surprise, the photographs met with stony scepticism from the ranks of the faithful.

Fairy laughter, effects. **Doyle** *addresses invisible committee.*

Doyle 'Gentlemen of the committee, this organisation exists to raise the profile of spiritualist researches away from the public perception of psychics and mediums as hoaxes. These fairies or earth spirits are being dismissed. But the earlier negatives were exhaustively examined and the technicians at Kodak have agreed there was no double exposure. I think you underestimate the innocence of the girls who took these pictures. These uneducated rural children had no skills or motives for deception. They sought no publicity. Indeed the photographs did not leave the family circle for a number of years. I'll fund a trip myself. I happily accept that the only person who should be permitted to touch the camera at any time would be an assistant whose qualifications would include deep scepticism on psychic matters.'

He turns to audience.

I arrived at the dell in Yorkshire shortly before noon in a splendid new motor car I had just purchased, a Napier tourer, which went like the wind. Miss Weegee Undine had elected to be the camera operator accompanying me, a self-confessed materialist and modern sceptic. She was also a remarkably beautiful young woman and rather forward. I put this down to the fact that since the war, love shared with her own generation was a scarce commodity.

Weegee – *in Edwardian motoring clothes, perhaps dust veils, camera tripod* – *coming into Cottingley dell, observed by* **Abraxas** *and* **Serena**, *who are partly concealed there.*

Doyle (*hushed*)   Miss Undine, this is the exact spot where
the fairies were photographed before. Five years before. I'm
sorry the car is so far away. I don't want to risk upsetting
entities by being parked too close.

Weegee   Assuming they don't meet a motor car, how long
are fairies meant to live?

Doyle   Fifteen hundred years, generally.

Weegee   I'd say this was a darling place to mount a vigil.
F.8 at a thirtieth of a second under this canopy. Do call me
Weegee, please, Sir Arthur. England in high summer, the
ground covered with woodland flowers. And I'm alone here
with a Lord. Oh wow! We should have a photograph of us
together. I could squeeze the shutter bulb with my naked
foot, or something.

Doyle   You should keep your voice down.

Weegee   Oh, I'm so sorry.

Doyle   We shouldn't speak here, unless it's absolutely
necessary.

Weegee   But if I see a fairy you'll have to pinch me on the
butt to make sure I'm not dreaming.

She sets up camera. **Doyle** *observes* **Serena** *with magnifying glass.*

Seen anything?

Doyle   A very unusual shrub.

Doyle *wanders away from her.*

Abraxas   We may not avoid a summons from the Seven
Immortals. You awoke as we were borne earthwards just
now, my eternal queen.

Serena   This spread of woodland where we shape
ourselves in matter is very fine, with the trees variously
green, yet well proportioned; under silver birches, look, high
summer calls up redcap mushrooms. Fount of ecstasy of the
ancients, whose fearless shamen drew truth from airy

trances – visiting other worlds and, nearby, little rivulets
which babble nurture to more sober souls, in the tongues of
little waterfalls, with banks of moss and dappled stones. Why
are we here?

Abraxas   We go to witness the planet's destruction by that
great evil, the Elect One of Darkness, my son Moloch.

Serena   Wherever we are, Abraxas, this is a better place
than where we were before, untroubled. But why did you
not wake me for your trial earlier? The Seven Immortals
could never have conscripted us from bliss if I could have
gone before them as your advocate. I would have poured
ashes on my head and rent my clothes.

Abraxas   The fact that Moloch was born from my most
regrettable act, a solitary pollution, cannot be contested in
front of the Seven. It is on the Akashic record.

Serena   And the record can be reinterpreted.
(*Posturing.*) 'It is true, my Lords, that the Archon here by my
side blinked once in the eternal night, and from that eddy in
the divine sight, a darkling thought grew; from a
momentary self-doubt. Who has not momentarily doubted
themselves? Each mortal does, not once but many times a
day; on average. My husband is the foremost being in
creation, but he is subject to the laws of creation, which
include the Law of Averages.'

Abraxas   If it had been spoken before the Seven, like the
loving spouse you are, then we should not be here. But I
have found out that this penance of ours could turn to our
advantage and become a gateway to the Ineffable realms,
where we would be troubled no more. There is a clause by
the Seven permitting transmigration to the Ineffable under
certain conditions. Make sure to be with me at the end, for
we go through to the Ineffable together, if at all.

Serena   This is not the first time I have heard how you
will pierce the final mystery of the Ineffable. How is the
present venture different?

Abraxas   This time, I am prepared.

Serena   You were prepared a thousand times before.

Abraxas   I am a thing that is and yet is not; an imaginary man. A fiction.

Serena   He doesn't sound as if he has a wife.

Abraxas   He does not have a wife; he has an assistant. I thought the author himself would do well enough. There he is, before us now. I summoned him.

Serena   Behold the writer!

She now examines **Doyle**. *Tweeting of birds.*

An author, outwardly calm and broad of back, but behold his mind – Look what strange and contrary beasts his imagination has a lease on: brownies, elves, gnomes, tree-devas, mannikins, cloud-fairies, hobgoblins and dancing sylphs.

Abraxas   You will have no difficulty in enchanting him.

Serena   Why should he need to be enchanted?

Abraxas   He needs to be brought on through time. He will be dead some while when it comes for the end of the earth.

Doyle *yawns. Immediately* **Weegee** *goes to him, seductive.*

Weegee   Isn't this the best sun-dappled mossy bank ever? Sir Arthur, I know you believe in fairies: what else do you believe in?

Doyle   Spiritualism. And decency.

Weegee   Oh my, look at all those spiders. And now I am going to lift up this spider by its thread, and put in on the petals of a buttercup, and now it's going on you! Oh, look, the back of your hand has got some pollen on it.

Doyle   Yes, from the snakeshead fritillary. Unmistakable scaly bronzed pattern, see? A common woodland dweller.

Weegee   Like a fairy bonnet. Sweet.

Doyle   Could you not talk, please.

Weegee   Sir Arthur. Do you believe in . . . free love?

Doyle   The very idea is a cruel device to rob womanhood of natural chastity. Hush now.

Weegee   But what about the fairies? Don't they put it around?

Doyle   Miss Undine, I am not an expert on the morals of fairies. Only an observer.

Weegee   Call me Weegee please.

Doyle   Weegee, stand by your camera.

Weegee   I hear what you're saying. I'll keep watch.

Weegee *goes to the camera.* **Serena** *goes and puts her influence over* **Doyle**, *magically.*

Abraxas   Serena, bring him to us so we make ourselves known.

Serena (*to* **Doyle**)   The horns of Elfland sound, far away. You see a throng disgorge from fairy courts under grass tussocks: a dazzling necklace, no higher than a jewelled snake, glides through the grass to ancient music, played by the courtiers on their tiny flutes and tabors: you see a procession of wimpled princesses just so high, in jonquil gowns on fairy palfreys, spindle-shanked, and shod in silver never banked. Doyle, follow us.

Doyle   I know you are illusion.

Serena   Do not resist us. Do not be difficult.

Doyle   I tried to follow you once under the hill, but you were gone, and now I have no time to follow. I have work to do. I am in my study, look, writing a medieval novel. I have all the research at my fingertips. The manuscript has to be

completed by midnight. Every time I finish a page, see, my
secretary dashes to the printers with it. Kindly let me alone.

*Sounds of crashing swordfights and expiring shrieks, interspersed with
the thunder of a typewriter as* **Doyle** *mimes typing to the noise.*
Weegee *takes the mimed pages one by one in a number of trips on
and offstage.*

Abraxas   As you type the final pages, your deerstalker hat
starts falling off its peg by the door. You hang it up, a
number of times, but then the Inverness cape in a corner of
the room starts getting a life of its own, making a number of
bids for escape, on one occasion flapping away emptily as
far as the hall. And on every occasion, on your return, the
large magnifying glass on your desk is in a different place.
Do you get the impression that something somewhere in the
universe is TRYING TO GET YOUR ATTENTION?

Serena   Would it not be easier to simply let him finish
what he is doing?

Abraxas   No! He's not the Creator, he's meant to be
helping the Creator. Typewriter! Get Qwerty! Seize up the
keys before his eyes, tangle them above the page, into a
lifeless leaden ball!

Weegee *waits for final page.*

Doyle (*to audience*)   My plans were almost skewered at the
last moment, when the Underwood Upright jammed
inexplicably. But hunting through my desk drawers, my
hand chanced on an ancient italic pen.

Abraxas   Damn me, he's incorrigible. He's at it again!

Doyle   Dashing it into the inkpot, I completed the final
sentences as the hall clock struck twelve. In high elation, I
picked up the inkwell, and threw it as hard as I can at the
wall. (*Shouts.*) 'I've done it!'

Weegee *exits with final page.*

Serena   He is ready. I will bring him.

Doyle   The inkwell shattered, and long fingers of ink started making their way rapidly down the wallpaper, but then slowed, as if time itself was having second thoughts. I become aware of a sort of buzzing, as if the insect of that particular moment was trapped, struggling to be free of its silken cocoon. The ink-fingers arrest their downwards rush and I found myself in the same sunlit glade in Cottingley. Two strange figures were in the glade.

Serena   Arthur Conan Doyle, we have been trying to get your attention for some time.

Doyle   I am sorry, madam. You have surprised me.

Serena   What of the summons from a silk-muffled silver trumpet, suspended in the air, in a seance in New York?

Doyle   I haven't been to New York for some months. I don't believe we've been introduced either.

Serena   The voice from the trumpet was very clear. It said, 'Serena, Queen of Heaven and Night, is to give you audience and instruction. Doyle, prepare to serve He Who Is Who He Is.'

Doyle   Have you seen my assistant at all, Miss Undine? I trust nothing untoward has happened to her.

Abraxas   So do I. But there are no signs of any foul play, are there? Can you see any crushed vegetation, broken stiletto heels, et cetera?

Serena   She's quite safe. She'll be back, in a twinkling.

Doyle   How do you know?

Serena   She is back in a further incarnation. Time will shortly pass, much time. You have been chosen to be Three Six Five's monitor on earth, at the end of earth's long day.

Doyle   Pardon my ignorance: who is Three Six Five?

Serena   The male principle of ourself. He stands before you now. The greatest of the Old Ones.

She unfurls the greenery from around **Abraxas** *who stands forth as Holmes.*

He revealed himself to the ancient Mesopotamians before the magus Zoroaster judged all liars to eternal fire. Three hundred and sixty-five star-studded Mesopotamian nights first made the length of a year. His priests charted the geometry of the skies, and planted the seed of consciousness in mankind. His thoughts are immeasurable. They dwarf the zoetropes of creation. The explosive birth, the implosive death of galaxies are all foretold in the superabundant consciousness of his brow! Abraxas is the god above gods, and takes precedence over all later manifestations of deity: Jehovah, Zeus, Mahomet and Krishna, all bow the knee and acknowledge his superiority.

Abraxas   How does this look to you?

Serena   He is also Ur-Archon Abraxas, but his names should not be uttered all together, or the fountains of the deep break up.

Doyle   I see. What are the fountains of the deep?

Abraxas   No man has seen them. They lie on the seabed, below where the freezing, inky river Styx outpours to Oceanus. The seas will rise together, by fifteen thousand cubits.

Doyle   How alarming. A scientific impossibility, of course.

Serena   Never mind what one-eyed Dame Science preaches. Three Six Five comes to earth in the final days, as prophesied, which is to say, celestically arranged, in a very small routine penance in giving birth to Moloch in a rash moment. You are to be his assistant. By the way, do instruct him if there are any infidelities to your work in this creation.

Doyle   There are so many internal errors in the tales themselves that fidelity was always problematic. And I should say to you now: I have done with Sherlock Holmes and foggy London streets. I've killed him off.

Serena   Unkill him off, then. You are a man of chivalrous instinct. Evil cannot triumph, unchallenged, even though it is the final days, long past your time.

Doyle   This must be a practical joke arranged by my old friend Harry Houdini – of course it is. (*Calls.*) Very funny, Harry. I'm calling your bluff! Come out now! (*Pause.*) I wonder how he knew I was in Cottingley, though?

Doyle *looks around the stage.*

Abraxas   Harry Houdini! If there were ever fairies behind these trees, they'd be weeping now. Harry's dead. Died a while back, after a blow to the solar plexus, from an over-athletic admirer, septic duodenum.

Doyle   Good Lord, you're right.

Abraxas   And he's not coming back, either. In the coffin, six-foot down, and Doctor Death's patent handcuffs have proved impossible for even Harry to unpick. After twenty-five years of fruitless seancing, even his faithful widow will have the eternal flame quenched on his grave: a shrewd and frugal move.

Doyle   Would it be possible to talk to him now?

Abraxas   Sadly Harry's lack of belief in the afterlife means he is now incommunicado.

Doyle   My dear late mother believed. Could you send her a message, saying –

Serena (*cross*)   We've already sent a message to your mother. She's happy that you are happy as a sandboy, and she is happy as a sandgirl.

Doyle   Did she really say 'sandgirl'?

Serena   She also said you would help us.

Pause.

Abraxas   Are you not a gentleman, Doyle? Sworn to protect the weaker sex?

Doyle   I would hope so.

Abraxas   This lady is an indivisible aspect of me, so you will be protecting her too. (*To* **Serena**.) He is no gentleman, if he refuses now. And if he claims to be a gentleman and is not, he lies. So we have him, either way.

Doyle   I do not lie.

Abraxas   You lie regularly, Doyle. The lies appear in print. Did you ever seek a retraction from *The Times* of London, which on the ninth of January 1923 opposite an advertisement for Cherry Blossom bootpolish, published the following: '"There are fairies" affirmed A. Conan Doyle.'?

Serena   'There are fairies', indeed!

Abraxas   My earliest representative, Magus Zoroaster cast liars into a lake of brimstone. Here's another statement you make, which is untrue. 'No women are ugly!' you have said, at least once a week, in the presence of witnesses too numerous to invoke. Now that's a lie.

Doyle   It's true.

Abraxas   Oh no, it's not. Ha, ha! Decent folk feel it *ought* to be true, but that's not the same, is it? Magus Zoroaster would have had you roasted for eternity, both sides. You are lucky to get off with a couple of days' light domestic service, answering the door and so forth, in Baker Street, before the world's end.

Doyle   When does the world end?

Abraxas   Oh, very shortly, now. Collision with a fifteen-million-ton meteorite, the bulk of which was spewed out and condensed when the earth was still a gaseous ball. Caledonia was wandering in space, until my dark son stumbled on her and accelerated her in the direction of her beginnings. Once, if you passed out through the Oört cloud's circumference, several lifetimes would pass before you would approach where Caledonia lay. Now she is closing fast, and through her long sojourn in the void, she has grown twice as big. Pelted by snowballs of methane, cloaked in interstellar grime and scooping up ammoniac shards of ice from comets' tails, she is now an unsteady confederacy of lethal matter, which Moloch has yoked together with a mesh of steel for single impact.

Doyle What kind of god are you, that lets these things happen?

Serena The kind who does solitary acts. His son also performed procreatively with the asteroid, which union hatched out two daughters into the starlight, sheltering them at first in caves hewn from glaciers of methane. But now Moloch has snatched his children from their mother's alkaline bosom, and the unfortunate offspring now find themselves bound for earth, where their father intends to violate them, as Caledonia herself arrives, adding his unborn incestuous offspring to the general sacrifice.

Arsile *and* **Morgue** *dance on, carrying sparklers for a dance around the stage. Music, Edge of Space.*

Serena Behold the adversary and his brood, as they outstrip Caledonia, coursing through hyperspace, in their etheric pod, to enact evil's own *festschrift*, the world's dark destiny!

Arsile/Morgue (*sing*) I'm not complaining, but planets
   all seem to be closer this year.
   Their faces mirrors of hope and despair
   Invading my dreams with low gravity schemes,
   Stars in my eyes say I'll never die,
   And yet nights into days flicker away.

Grow lights to see **Moloch** *with a long tail coming out of his jodhpurs.*

Arsile/Morgue (*sing*) No one goes up after they drown
   And yet it goes round with never a sound.
   I'm not complaining, not even in training
   Cos I got four feet on the ground.

Arsile *and* **Morgue** *are clad in extravagantly bad-taste trailer-trash rag-doll punk. They subside after their song.*

Moloch   Remember, Arsile and Morgue, when you are on earth, the daughter of a Moloch always walks upright on its rear legs. Otherwise, people will think you're reverting.

Arsile   We got space sickness. We wanna go home!!

Morgue   Why did you pluck us from the only home we knew, Father?

Moloch   You'd be puking more than your rings, back on Caledonia. I left the nursery airlock open.

Arsile   Why do we need to get to earth ahead of momma?

Moloch   It will become clear in due course. Trust me. You're on course and there's nothing you need do. Indeed, there's nothing you can do about that! And you don't have to wait long for the rest of your education. As soon as the pod crosses into the earth's radio footprint, the tv in the corner will activate, and you can receive reassuring, step-by-step bulletins on how I am taking charge.

Morgue   When we arrive, will the earthlings not resent you and hurt us?

Moloch   You'll pass till I find you, easy. It's the minerals in your mother's soil which give you your cast-iron disguise. It's easy for you – I've had to chomp on gravel picked up from round Ayres Rock every day so I can blend in.

Morgue   If our mother was from earth, doesn't that make us a wee bit human?

Moloch   Naa. You soaked up the local dialogue preferences through the molecular lattice in your cubation pods. No trace of arsewipe humanity gets through.

Arsile   I'm still missing mother.

Moloch   You can't miss what you never had.

Morgue   It's not fair. How can we not have a mother, with all our feelings about her?

Moloch   Look at me. I don't have a mother. You don't need one!

Arsile   When it rained ammonia we used to think mother was in a bad mood with you for going off, as we wandered through space. Lava would boil up inside our cave, poison the air, and everything would shuggle.

Moloch   She became chemically more active, sure, when I shifted her out of deep space. Passing solar systems always used to upset her insides. I had to lash her together, she was so unstable.

Arsile   We used to pretend the explosions were her way of saying she loved us, and we were her favourites and she was actually beautiful, with long black hair, and a pale face like a sexy witch.

Moloch   Next time you're in the dunney take a good look astern through the porthole. Caledonia is about fifteen kilometres wide with two volcanic cones of ammonia and hydrogen cyanide which only look like tits a hundred miles away! It was a nightmare getting you two started. I had to go to earth and do a lengthy infant genocide programme to get in the mood.

Arsile   What's an infant?

Moloch   Oh, who's not doing their homework, Morgue? Hint. Molochs bypass that stage, emerging as fully-formed adults in many regards. And . . . I gotta downsize to one when I get to Oz. There's just time to show you before I pop off. The Toltec Indians knew me as Chac-Mool and the women would do – what? Look, they're offering up their . . .

Moloch *makes an area with his hands into which the girls stare.*

Arsile   . . . 'Infants'?

Moloch   To me. Good girl . . . They start off small, without hard-wired speech centres. The naked blokes opening up the little preverbals, with old-fashioned lapis lazuli blades, see, are my temple priests.

Morgue   What sex are temple priests?

Arsile   Male. Tackle in front, look.

Moloch   Go in close on the man. Focus on the fresh blood. Put the magnification up three hundred and sixty-five, what do you see now?

Morgue   A wiggly thing.

Moloch   It's a cheeky little piece of microbiology, a malaria virus. Even when they work out how it goes, it still will kill more human 'infants' than everything else I've thrown at them! To end up, some holiday snaps to show you what a fun time you can have on earth. There's me crossing the Bering Strait in a kayak sewn from human skins. Now I'm in Persia, where I got the Zoroastrians to make war on me. The Tigris and the Euphrates were so choked with human bodies, look, even the crocs look like they got indigestion. And here I am at the end of my long trek – outside Jerusalem setting my temple up in the valley of Hinnom.

Arsile   Is that a ziggurat there made up of human skulls?

Moloch   Yeah. Look close and you'll see they're *baby* skulls! (*Beat.*) Right. Arsile and Morgue! We're passing the Two Ravens, which is a double neutron star and I don't have to remind you the gravitational field is the ideal personal accelerator. I do a backflip out of here, a figure-of-eight slingshot round the Ravens, and I'm on my way. Get there twenty earth years before you arrive. Who says I'm not a good dad, eh?

Morgue   Why don't you use the black hole for a slingshot, instead?

Moloch   Black hole surfing at my time of life? I couldn't
keep above the event horizon. I'd miss the earth by a mile
and I'd come back in here a one-eyed mermaid with
alopecia. You got to realise I did my back in permanently,
getting you two started.

Arsile   How did you do it? Get us started?

Morgue   He laid on his back and put his tail in a hole.

Arsile   Is it true, when we get us pregnant, the little
puppies, when they're ready, eat their way out of us?

Moloch   Don't worry, I can bite their heads off so fast
they'll never get a chance to gang up on you.

Morgue   Why should we have them at all?

Moloch   I gotta go, because at this very moment, a
dingo's dragging an infant out of its buggy which is parked
under a bottlebrush outside the Little Bethlehem
launderette in Brisbane. I'm going to downsize, and crawl
into the stroller instead before the junkie mum comes back –
look, there she is, cashmere cardie and fuck-me pumps,
going down on the pharmacist in his car – lost her
prescription, again! I'm going to be suckled on PCP,
synthetic heroin and God knows what other crap she's
pumping. But it's worth it for the ID, and it always fools
'em; the old changeling routine can't be beat!

Moloch *exits*.

Morgue   It's all right for him being so cheerful, but what
have we got to look forward to?

Arsile   I tell you what we've got. Daddy, waiting for us on
earth!

Morgue   Waiting to put his tail in us.

Arsile   And then, pregnant Moloch bitches *die*, because
the kids all come out together. The mothers explode in this
cannibal frenzy of wains, where the pup that wins eats the

rest, so it gets big enough to eat you. In ten minutes you're just a red smear on the wallpaper.

Morgue   Let's make a spell to *refuse* father's tail.

Arsile   Like how?

Morgue   He will lose what makes him male
  A bloody stump, and he looks so pale –

Arsile/Morgue   Father's lost it, screams and wails,
  And plastic surgeons, they all fail.

Morgue *and* **Arsile** *exit to music. Lights move to* **Doyle**, **Abraxas** *and* **Serena**.

Abraxas   'All that is necessary for the forces of evil to win, is for good men to do nothing,' the statesman wrote. You would agree with the noble sentiments of Edmund Burke, would you not, Doyle? Will you not harken to the voice of conscience, and help combat evil?

Doyle   It seems I have no choice.

Abraxas   Excellent fellow! Let us go forth like knights of old, to Baker Street! Serena! Till tomorrow at midnight!

Serena   Till tomorrow night!

Abraxas   What will you do here?

Serena   This glade is even more ravishing in the future than it was in the past, if that were possible. When we came first, there were no spiders! All this must be recorded. My dissertation will distil the secrets of its beauty down the ages.

Abraxas   To what end?

Serena   The end is a slender primrose-tinted phial of distillate of nature's beauty, shaped like a lens, which I'll present to Moloch, bowing low, saying 'I need no thanks for this. Only glance once upon paradise through this medium. Then you would not find it in yourself to destroy this planet.'

Abraxas   I wish your advocacy well, but in the unlikely event of it swaying Moloch, the game is up for us here, have you thought of that? If he repents, we will be recalled and we can never hope to gain the Ineffable unobserved.

Serena   I believe we will never gain the Ineffable together. I have observed so many spiders, everywhere. Fearless global navigators, clinging to single strands who net their next destiny from the wind. Ascending and descending like Jacob's angels, so each fresh morning, the sun discovers the dewed, discarded threads of these intrepid stratonauts in millions, silvering the grass. To my task –

Serena *collects invisible spider threads and exits.*

Abraxas   That's it; we have lost her for the duration.

Doyle   Lost Serena? How?

Abraxas   The sugar spider was after your time. Arachnidus sucrosus is now an epidemic in Britain, since the farmers grow little else but sugar cane. Its bite induces madness.

Weegee *arrives bearing the camera as before and sets it up on its tripod. She is futuristically dressed, with a number of electronic leads implanted in her, which grow in number each time she appears.*

Abraxas   Moloch put a genetically engineered hydrocarbon converter enzyme into the spider's airborne thread. This airborne thread, wherever it alighted, turned all fossil fuels to sugar. Every coalface became a mass of sucrose, and every oil well in the world jammed with the oozings of crude black strap molasses. The sugar spiders continued to prosper and adapted later after petrol disappeared and low-temperature-tolerant sugar cane became the energy crop for farmers, as far as the Arctic Circle.

Doyle   What have you done to Weegee?

Abraxas   I have not touched her. She has reincarnated, and will not know you. New to this earth again, she now is

Moloch's foremost indentured serf, blind in her ambition to
his intentions, even on the eve of destruction.

Weegee   Hey, old-timer! You haven't seen anything grey
with almond eyes drop through the trees? Seen any aliens
hereabouts? They're meant to have landed near here and
Mr Moloch's sent me out to get photographs. Don't see why
he can't fake them, since he never lets truth get in the way
of a good story. But if the world's ending, this is the last
chance to qualify for the top level of journalistic control. I'd
chop out my own ovaries with a meat cleaver and pass them
over to the first caller, to be selected for the Informational
Matrix. See these leads on my hands? The more you have
on, the closer you are to qualifying.

Doyle   What do the leads do?

Weegee   They take the signature of your vital intelligence,
and then suddenly, you're in there with the elite. Only a few
thousand ever make it. They say it's like making out with
God, that wouldn't be too bad, would it, even for thirty-six
hours. Or however much time is left.

Doyle   When exactly is the world to be destroyed?

Weegee   Twelve midnight, tomorrow. The skies will
darken and fill the howling air with smoke thicker than a
thousand volcanoes. Or that's what it said yesterday in the
Thistle, the last paper on the face of the planet that Mr
Moloch didn't own – till today. All growth from vegetation
will cease as dust storms in the upper air cut us off from the
sun. 'Count them blessed those who do not survive the tidal
wave after the impact. The last rituals of humanity are most
like to be stark cannibalism, as the survivors devour each
other in some darkling cave.' The seas are all going to drain
away to salt pans, as the water gets locked up in domes of
ice at the poles.

Doyle   Pardon my ignorance, but isn't there some country
who could muster their military might to do something:
such as fire a salvo from supercharged twenty-four-inch

naval guns at the incoming meteorite to break it up into fragments?

Weegee   There've been no big guns, and no navies in the world since I was born. Do you have Alzheimer's disease? Stupid question. You wouldn't know if you did.

Doyle   I'm surprised that a great power, such as Britain, or indeed the United States hasn't declared a state of emergency –

Weegee   Where *are* your memory pills? America's long gone. It's history. The States all got disunited by Mr Moloch, though they did get to keep their personal weapons. But even if they fire their Colt 45s all together, it won't make much difference, will it? Did you know Sherlock Holmes is meant to appear at the end of all things?

Doyle   I did, matter of fact.

Weegee   Well, there he is. Confirmation. Right behind you! (*To* **Abraxas**.) Could I trouble you for a photograph, sir? You never know, the paper's policy could change.

Abraxas   No trouble. Delighted. I always like to have my likeness taken.

Weegee *positions camera to take picture of* **Abraxas**.

Abraxas   What do you think of this asteroid scare, then?

Weegee   I was going to ask you. I thought you'd know.

Abraxas   You tell me. I've only just arrived.

Weegee   If this situation was really serious, I would have thought Mr Moloch would be doing something about it. Trouble is, if Mr Moloch's got a blind spot, it is that he's really not that interested in space. I've noticed he doesn't care when communication satellites fall down. Now that's the photo done. If I run across the field now I could drop you off a print so you could have it even if the paper decides you're not news.

Abraxas   You're too kind.

Doyle   Look out for spiders. I hear one has a terrible bite.

Weegee   Arachnidus sucrosus? I was inoculated before my Matrix exams. If you're on the fast track for promotion all that stuff is free.

Weegee *exits with plate from camera.*

Doyle   Is it wise to announce your arrival so soon to the other camp by leaving your likeness?

Abraxas   You'll see, he'll never guess it's me.

Doyle   You were telling me about the sugar cane spider. What happened to the motor car?

Abraxas   It disappeared overnight. Since the car had been responsible for forty million deaths in the twentieth century alone, Moloch, who had made no secret of the first part of his spider's stratagem, was cast as a saviour. (*A thunderclap.*) That is the pathenogenetic daughters' travel pod, breaking up the stratosphere; they will join us very shortly.

Doyle   Weegee has missed her scoop, then.

Abraxas   Quite a perilous assignment for a single young woman. They could eat her if she got too close. They may be ripening against their will, but at oestrus, the female Moloch's desire for flesh becomes overpowering. You should remember to lie down if they come this way. If you keep as still as possible, they may leave you for carrion. Either that, or you could pretend you had been bitten by spiders.

Doyle   Should something not be done about Serena's safety?

Abraxas   Serena will have fallen to the spider's stratagem. They work for my son.

Doyle   Are you saying that Moloch has plotted to poison Serena and driven her mad?

Abraxas   It would have been very little trouble to Moloch
to add some dedicated hallucinogenic toxins to the spider's
bite, and specify the exact delirium into which a chosen
victim will fall.

Doyle   Why should he do that to her?

Abraxas   Nothing would be more pleasant for him than
to torture me at one remove by putting my other half
through humiliating torments. As Serena dances through
the sugar cane praising creation, threads will softly caress
her. Very soon, she will be lulled into discarding her own
finery woven of the finest silk – heavenly bombyx
caterpillars' spume – for it will feel coarse and inferior
beside this earth product – the innocent-seeming woodland
raiment – and she will dress herself in spiderwebs.

Enter **Morgue** *and* **Arsile**. **Doyle** *lies down on his back.*

Arsile   I don't like this planet. You land with a bump and
then you can't see the curve in the horizon. Maybe I'd feel
better if I have something to eat –

Morgue   Arsile – Come and look at this! (**Doyle**,
recumbent.)

Arsile   He's making babies.

Morgue (*excited*)   He's never!

Arsile   Is this not just how father brought us about? He
put his tail in the ground, laid down on his back and
wheeshed away.

Morgue   This one must have finished. He's not jigging.

Arsile   Let's see if he's done.

They roll **Doyle** *over.*

Morgue   He's human. But he'll do.

Enter **Serena**, *staggering, dressed in spiderwebs.*

Serena   The spiders stung me. They stung me all at once with a thousand needles – help me. Help me. (*She collapses.*) Get them off me! Eugh!

Serena *brushes at the webs feebly.*

Abraxas   Careful now, the sugar spiders have poisoned this one, too, look. His gaze, look, traps only phantoms; tiny equivocators, who whistle through the windsock of his soul.

Arsile   He looks sane enough to me.

Abraxas   The very early stages of dementia.

Arsile   My stomach thinks my throat is slit. Where can we get satisfaction?

Abraxas   You may think I am being timid about offering myself, but you should know your father already has scouts in this area, looking for you.

Arsile   Father? Come on, Morgue, let's run home and hide from him.

Morgue   Where's home?

Arsile   Scotland. And get that grey gluey keck off your scut or you'll go crazy too –

Exit **Arsile** *and* **Morgue**. **Doyle** *stands up.* **Serena** *writhes.*

Abraxas   By George, Doyle, you had a narrow escape there. I'd forgotten that the Moloch can see what's in the mind of its dinner. Lucky Serena arrived.

Doyle   Is there a remedy?

Abraxas   None; for thirty-six and a half hours, the sufferer is driven to invention and madly improvises some arbitrary history.

Serena *pretends to ride a horse.*

Abraxas   A mincing miniature, in the vanguard of a fairy ride: which is to say she does not exist, except for lunatics. I'm sure you know her well.

Serena *stops riding and approaches; begs from* **Doyle**, *lewdly and suggestively.*

Abraxas   And now the Queen of the Fairies turns woman of the town, selling herself for pennies in the street.

Doyle (*fleeing*)   Madam, this will not do.

Serena, *rejected, mimes a straitjacket and gag.*

Abraxas   Now she is prisoner.

Doyle   I wonder if she knows how her mind has run away. (*Approaches.*) Serena? Do you know your name, madam?

Abraxas   See? Not a flicker.

Serena   Of course I know my name. Serena. I hate it, that is all, because I hate myself. I hate myself because I hate the world, which was created by a very wicked god, all for his pleasure in suffering. And this god in his wisdom has seen to it that Moloch, a devilish presence, married me and delights to see me shackled and if I am not smeared daily in my own excrement in protest, why, he kindly provides his own. Is that not why you have come, gentlemen? You do this to me every day, do you not? Quickly now. Get it over with, and then chain me again, in my solitary cell.

Doyle   She thinks she is imprisoned, married to your son. You are not in prison, here, but open air, amongst trees you delighted in openly just now. Look up, the sky is blue.

Serena   The sky spits devils anywhere I walk. You lie, here is a wall.

Abraxas   You're very gallant, Doyle, but you can do nothing for her.

Doyle   Try pushing your hand through it, madam.

Serena *does so in mime, fails to pass wall.* **Doyle** *impulsively picks her up and carries her through the invisible wall and puts her down the other side.*

Doyle   You are free.

Serena   How did you do that? Work miracles?

Doyle   And this is your consort, madam.

Weegee (*off*)   Professor Holmes!

Serena (*to Doyle*)   You did well to free me, but it is past belief that I could be married to this man.

Weegee *enters with photo; gives it to* **Abraxas**.

Weegee   Something very strange, Professor. The photograph is not of you, sir.

Serena   Professor Holmes. You see? A confirmed bachelor.

Weegee   The negatives must have been switched. I have to go – the aliens have been seen heading north.

Exit **Weegee**.

Doyle   Star clusters, nebulae and galaxies.

Abraxas *tears up photo*.

Doyle   What does this mean?

Abraxas   I was transmitting on the wrong wavelength. Pity, I would have liked to see how I look.

Doyle   What is your husband's name, madam?

Serena   Moloch is my tormentor-husband's name, for the second time.

Doyle   How long do you think – how long have you been married to Mr Moloch, Serena?

Serena   Twenty years. For all that time, I have been imprisoned in an upper chamber at our house. I have been constantly defiled. I was not even allowed to cut my own wrists, when he murdered our little children in front of me.

Doyle   When did he commit these murders?

Serena When they were babies, after he had raped them. And then he dragged them both outside the house, cracked their skulls open and ate the brains.

Doyle Where is this house?

Serena Far to the south, on a plain with imported trees and grossly and cruelly mutated animals. That is his other amusement. Two-headed hyenas.

Doyle In England?

Serena Yes, but closer to a replication of Africa, now. Near the house were handsome settlements; towns had stood for a thousand years, but at my husband's nod the wreckers threw them down.

Doyle Serena, do you truly believe that you are not, nor have ever been, this man's consort?

Pause.

Serena No, I have never been married to Sherlock Holmes. But I will kiss his feet. (*She does so.*) If he is here, we must be close to deliverance. Either he will save us, or these are the final days, and he heralds my release from cruelty.

Doyle How did you arrive in Cottingley?

Serena It must have been when I heard about the meteorite. That gave me the strength. I heard of a man who can save us all. My husband can make that happen, if he repudiates what lies in his black heart. That girl can take me to him, can't she?

Serena *exits.*

Abraxas Hitching a ride from Weegee is a rather perilous undertaking.

Doyle How so?

Abraxas The steam-powered Wattcopter has such poor power-to-weight ratio that even without a passenger on

board, I imagine Weegee will hardly be able to clear
Hadrian's Wall, without knocking off a layer of stones.

*Huffing and puffing: a model of a Heath Robinson-like flying
contraption flies, with a model Weegee pilot and Serena passenger.*

Doyle Is this world now entirely without petrol?

Abraxas There are, they say, still uncontaminated flasks
in a laboratory in China. But Weegee's taken pity on her, so
let's follow them. We will use the rapid travel mode of
Tibetan monks who can cover long distances between
monasteries effortlessly, with a bounding run which reduces
effective body weight by self-hypnosis. This is completely
safe unless attempted by those with a history of cardio-
vascular problems or allergies to ancient oriental wisdom.
Do exactly as I do. Ignoring the varied topography of North
England, fix the mind on the middle distance . . . And now,
the invocation to become a dweller on the threshold of
matter by allowing the illumination of almighty Buddha to
rouse the chakras, one by one . . . Aum! Repeat after me.
Aum!

Doyle Aum! Aum! Aum!

Abraxas Red! Orange! Yellow! Green! Blue! White!
Number Seven, crown chakra, open! Divine vision, on!
One-seventh gravity pedestrian mode, commence!

Lighting change. **Abraxas** *does an exaggerated stride on the spot.*
Doyle *imitates. Music, Edge of Space. Effects.*

Abraxas Don't concentrate too hard or you'll shoot
upwards, and never be seen again. Until the Chinese
invasion, uncontrolled levitation was the most frequent
cause of death among Tibetans living at altitudes above
three thousand six hundred and fifty metres. They just fly
away; like ladybirds. It's a little known statistic because
observers are rare on the roof of the world: but you have my
word for it.

Doyle   Abraxas, I know it may matter very little to you . . .
what happens to me at the end of the world?

Abraxas   Don't worry! I'm looking after you, because I
like you, Doyle. I should have made more of you. Like
beetles. Maybe not. I made plenty of beetles, but then
they're smaller than you. The instant the meteorite hits, you
may invoke the Seven Immortals by name, and they will
transplant you back to within three hundred metres of your
car, and you may not be able to account for an hour or so.
As the years pass you may be tempted to discount this
experience, because you are unable to place it. My advice to
you with baffling experience is accept them as part of your
spiritual path. This is not a dream. In dreams, people can't
look at their hands or toes. (**Doyle** *does this.*) Apart from
minor wiring trouble with the nearside headlight which your
garage should be able to rectify, your fast and powerful
Napier will give you yeoman service. You like zooming
around at speed, don't you! Yes, I can tell! I can see you
doing it for the rest of your life! And you believe in fairies
too! In fact, you die, believing in fairies. What delicious
contradictions humanity is made up of!

Doyle   And the names of the Seven Immortals are . . .?

Abraxas   There is a little word trick I used to remember
them. You should memorise it as well. 'If India slams into
Asia, Tibet rises, Everest catches a cobweb, the earth cools'
– wait, that's climate and plate techtonics, not mnemonics.
Damn. Where were we? Tibet, Buddhism – all seeing
Buddha, doo-da, doo-da, Kempton racetrack five miles long
– no, I've lost it. Oh dear! I need to keep my wits about me.
Because I'm trying to get out, too, you know, even though
the Seven Immortals have made it so damnably hard. The
get-out clause appears to have been written by the same
gang who designed the Gordian knot. Get a load of this. I
have to quote, 'Be consumed by the virgin seed of the dark
word' in order to get to the Ineffable. And now I foresee
you're going to ask me what the Ineffable is.

Doyle   I thought you weren't allowed to foresee.

Abraxas   Fair enough. I deduce. (*Points.*) There go
Moloch's daughters. But swift as cheetahs, or Diana's
hounds, they will not escape their father if they go that way!
(*Beat.*) The Ineffable is that of which one cannot speak,
something that goes beyond time and eternity and even
godhead itself. Even as Supreme Being, one is still chained
to the tedious soap opera of Matter; desire begets being, and
being begets bathos, et cetera. Nobody learns anything at
this level, because nobody can. In the swamp of existence,
the bullfrog starts as a teeny tadpole, grows up, gets a big
idea and then inflates itself till it bursts. The ripples of the
explosion spread, the water goes quiet for a moment, the
black hole covers over with pond weed, then the damn thing
happens all over again, with another friggin' tadpole
somewhere else, with no one any wiser.

Consider the star map I accidentally generated. Millions of
collisions! Anywhere in space, wait long enough, kaboum!
The universe is one big pile-up. It is only the tragically short
life of that self-deluding worm, Man, that prevents the
species seeing that the game's just not worth the candle. As
for being saddled with the job of creator: why should
anyone want it? Everyone always blames everything that
goes wrong on you. So while I am nominally doing penance
here, invigilating the evil one's plans to munch his way
through the full picnic hamper of humanity's squeaking
souls, at the same time, I am trying to work out how to get
myself and my better half to – Oh, I say. Almost overshot.
Weegee is being flagged to land. Gently resume the
sevenfold mantle of full gravity as you allow the landscape
about you to come into focus.

Halts, looks round.

Below are valleys of green cane, while all around us on the
uplands is knee-high purple heather bisected by intermittent
coveys of small brown birds hugging the contours of the hill.
(*Distant popping of guns.*) If we accept the world's cruel master

is somewhere near, we can now assign the gunfire reports –
pump action twelve-bore, number six shot, cordite
propellant – to directors of the Thistle News group, who will
be taking potshots at fleeing grouse, while awaiting the
arrival of the large bribe that induced their betrayal of their
shareholders. Nothing changes, does it? I fear the only thing
that is going to stop this sort of corrupt collusion between
the fourth estate and big business is a large meteorite.

Doyle   Abraxas – I know it's not meant to be till
tomorrow but something already appears to be coming
between the earth and the sun.

Abraxas   Only the moon. Caledonia is still a million miles
away. But the moon herself will serve our purpose well
enough: under the cloak of the eclipse we may eavesdrop on
the enemy.

We see a moon, huge, black, with the sun's corona behind it flaming.

But not too close, for the eclipse will be interrupted – a
pious soul, a Russian Old Believer will shortly light himself
up and from Siberia attempt to beam a great wattage to
Scotland.

Doyle   How does he plan to bend light round the globe?

Abraxas   With a solar reflector. Before humanity's
interests were captured and pointed inward, mighty sails of
silver foil unfolded over the poles, banishing night for ever
from wintry Alaskan towns.

Doyle   You say this man himself lights up? Is this achieved
as a result of his religious beliefs?

Abraxas   Why should there be any connection to his
beliefs? The Northern Lights, sea plankton phosphorescing,
the sparks from the rutting firefly are not regarded as
religious miracles, are they?

Enter **Moloch** *in a kilt, accompanied by* **Weegee**, *in goggles,
carrying a big space-age machine pistol with a huge belt made up of
hypodermic syringes, standing by him importantly as loyal lieutenant.*

Moloch (*speech*)   Thistle shareholders! Your paper and your proud reputation for independence is safe in my hands because truly I am one of you. My family tree shows unequivocally my penniless and innocent ancestors were forced from these moors in the Highland clearances. These innocent landless victims of greed were then criminalised by society before being arrested and abused, reamed out before the mast, halfway round the world, to Norfolk Island penal colony. And now the long-lost son returns. Caledonia, I am putting money into your economy; fertilising the matriarchal sod with showers of gold with the very able assistance of my management team. Oh! Mother, don't fret, because very soon the rest of you will be coming home, too. For now, I embrace these slopes, your breasts, modestly clad now, in purple haze of heather but which I will adore even more, when it is stripped to the rocks.

Fondles **Weegee** *who is standing to attention.*

Doyle   He should not be permitted to do this to a lady!

Abraxas   A lady would have surely picked up the reference to loss of topsoil after impact. Weegee has nothing in common with a lady. She believes one thing only, that to serve her master is to satisfy her ambition.

Weegee   Long live Celestial Communications Incorporated!

Doyle   Even so, he is a swine!

Moloch   Caledonia, be naked for me now as the shadow falls, if not in reality yet, then in the bedchamber of my imagination.

Moloch *moves from kissing* **Weegee** *to kiss the earth as* **Serena** *enters.*

Serena   Moloch. Moloch!

Moloch   It's the wifelet! What are you doing out of doors, darling? How long has it been, since you stepped outside? Twenty years?

Serena   Twenty years.

Doyle   Wifelet! He connives with her delusions. Confirming his spiders were the ones that created her present reality.

Abraxas (*dry*)   Well done, Doyle.

Moloch   Off you go, Weegee.

Exit **Weegee**.

Serena   What mischief is Weegee performing for you now?

Moloch   Those darts are just so the aliens don't panic and hurt themselves when they're captured. If you tried to stop them with your bare hands, they'll bite your arse out. You're welcome to try. What do you want?

Serena   I want you to take action. It may be too late, but you have to do something. You must. Sherlock Holmes has been seen.

Moloch   The photograph didn't come out. As for the reports in the papers, the *Thistle* was scaremongering, trying to boost circulation so I'd pay more for a controlling share.

Serena   The lies fall ever thicker. I know what you are. You have no innocence. Only cunning. It is dark wherever you tread.

Moloch   Give a dog a bad name! There just happens to be an eclipse here, that's all.

Serena   The great crime of the coming days was foreshadowed long ago. I know where they are buried. The bodies of our little ones.

Moloch   Bollocks! We never had any children. You're barmy. I could get the best detective in the world and you'd still not believe my innocence.

Serena   Then get Sherlock Holmes to investigate you.

Moloch   Fine, you got him. While he's on the job, get him to prove I'm plotting the end of the world, too. Why should I want the world to end, when I own it?

Serena   Why was there no intelligence of disaster anywhere till yesterday? I don't know why you want this frightful thing. Nobody knows anything any more. It is as if you have contrived a fog of universal stupidity in which you can do what you want.

Moloch   I didn't have to contrive anything, the fog was there already.

Serena   Why has astronomy withered on the vine? Where are the telescopes that could have predicted this?

A green spotlight suddenly on **Moloch**.

Moloch   Now just a minute. Something funny is definitely going on up there.

Serena   That radiance is from a Russian holy man. Sergei sends this light to you with a blessing. He is sitting in the parabola of a solar furnace, half a world away.

Moloch   Yeah, cross-legged with a floral necklace and a silly smile on his mush.

Serena   He has chosen a harmless piece of the spectrum to demonstrate. He could incinerate you in a second, if he chose.

Moloch   No one threatens me!

Serena   He is not threatening you. He is showing how he can vaporise frozen gases and cause the asteroid to explode or change course.

Moloch   Tell him to point himself at Caledonia then, I don't need a green spotlight following me round like I was a pantomime King Rat.

Serena   Sergei says the atmosphere will weaken his rays too much if he tries from earth. He needs to get close.

Moloch   Now this all suddenly rings a bell. This is the bloke who propped up the Siberian mobsters' pay-TV till I came along. I don't remember him as religious. They used him to fry anyone late with the money between two fingers. Then still on-camera, he'd screw these big Archangel hookers, their hair would stand on end and you'd see St Elmo's fire playing over spotted backsides the size of the Kremlin Wall! I got it. I could give him his own cooking programme. He could prong a llama, and barbecue it at the same time.

Serena   Sergei is offering his God-given gifts and his life, if necessary, to save the world before it is too late! You have to get him into space; somehow. He doesn't want one of your disgusting cooking programmes!

Moloch   It may be disgusting to you, but it's what goes on, and has done from time immemorial. In fact, I used to watch Abraham in his temple, the other side of the valley Hinnom, filling the woolly ones from behind, regular as clockwork, as he cut the animals' throats.

Serena   Your lies are starting again. Your pathological lies.

Moloch (*calls*)   Oy, Sergei turn it up! It's so dark now I can't see which brown envelope is for the Thistle chairman!

Serena   Look at you, drunk on the prospect of extinction. I've done what I can. I now realise there is no hope. I suppose the death of hope gives you some pleasure.

Moloch   Wrong again. I was thinking. As it happens I have a genuine, working communications launch unit in London left over from the old days, when I religiously replaced satellites every time one got knocked out by Neil Armstrong's frozen piss.

Serena   So what is your excuse for not sending Sergei up?

Moloch   No worries. He can go up atop a satellite rocket. I'll get Weegee to blag a spacesuit from the British Museum.

I give you my word. As a fall-back, there's also another rocket in the barn, behind the house, we could use – if the touchpaper still lights, after two decades of chickenshit.

Music, Edge of Space. Light changes to pink as **Weegee** *enters with* **Arsile** *and* **Morgue** *handcuffed, with hypodermic syringes imbedded all over them, like porcupines.* **Weegee** *behind, the triumphant jailer with the pistol. As soon as* **Moloch** *approaches* **Arsile** *or* **Morgue** *they try and bite him.*

Moloch   I'm adopting these two frisky female aliens as the latest extension to the Melchester wildlife park. They know me better than they pretend – I name them – Arsile and Morgue – Hey, gently now, I'm not your dinner! Have I got surprises for you! I'm going to spoil you rotten! You'll go to Harrods tomorrow, girlies, and you can have anything that catches your eye – but you gotta behave and do what your daddy says. I'm going to have two beds made up in my dressing room – so they can become accustomed to the delights of civilisation.

Serena   No! Stop! They must not be allowed to be near him!

Moloch   I'm not turning them out into the park yet! They've come from a completely sterile environment. They could catch something very nasty, and then my darlings would have to be pumped full of all sorts of things, steroids and antibiotics . . .

Serena   You're not going to spend a minute alone with them. I'm going to be watching you night and day.

Moloch   I don't think sleep deprivation is a very good idea, Serena, for someone in your condition. Weegee! Make this the headline news tonight and park anything on Caledonia past the watershed.

Weegee   Yessir!

Moloch   Humanity may be threatened, sir, but that should not stop our heartfelt rejoicing that the family of

Man is not alone in the universe, blah blah. Tie it in with an entertainment programme. Empty the prisons! Not a single murderer or nonce remains behind bars tonight: from now on, every whore and rent boy is on the street. And in honour of Sherlock Holmes' homecoming, have fleets of steam pantechnicons tip cocaine till it fills Trafalgar Square!

Exit **Moloch**, **Serena**, **Sergei**, **Weegee** *pushing the twins off, snarling and twisting. Lights going slowly back to normal.*

Doyle   I find it hard to restrain myself, watching Serena being humiliated.

Abraxas   Have you thought how much harder I find it to stop myself leaping to her rescue? But we must use brains, not fists. And all is not lost. Our enemy may not be 'all there'.

Doyle   What do you mean, he's a lunatic?

Abraxas   That green stain on the seat of Mr Moloch's kilt; what does it whisper to you? It says to me he may have been 'cut' to tidy him up, when he was a little changeling.

Doyle   A green stain also might say he had slipped on some grass.

Abraxas   No no. This is a single round patch of intense regular colour, which is an exact spectroscopic match for Moloch propagator. What we may be seeing is seepage from the inexpertly amputated organ's stump.

Doyle   It could be an eccentric addition to the Moloch family tartan.

Abraxas   No, no. I believe he is now handicapped. If so, it follows he won't be able to force himself on his daughters in the traditionally approved manner –

He removes a cellphone from his pocket and passes it to **Doyle**.

The Edinburgh medical college where you trained has become a world centre for plastic surgery. Ask for a search of the southern hemisphere database for all remedial cosmetic operations over the last fifty years. Tell the medical librarians to get the records in a cabriolet to Waverley Station, Edinburgh, in time for the 8.10 sleeper train to Euston. Any trouble, just tell them who you are.

Doyle   A call from a long-dead writer will be treated as a prank.

Abraxas   I meant, tell them that you are Dr Watson.

Doyle   If this is as important as you believe, should it be discussed at all over the telephone?

Abraxas (*takes phone back*)   Very well, since we are getting so security conscious, ignoring the galloping passage of time, I'll go to Edinburgh myself and see what I can gather up. You go straight to Baker Street and get a good night's sleep, so you can be fresh tomorrow. The housekeeper will wake you with a cup of her very best tea, at seven forty-three tomorrow morning, before she goes to Mass, in that dreadful black coat of hers with the fake-fur astrakhan collar. Do help yourself to one of the kippers for breakfast. Then pick up a copy of every newspaper from the newsagent's downstairs. That is very important, all right? Every paper. We need to know which lies Moloch wants us to believe.

Doyle   What about the errors Serena fears may creep in if you are left alone?

Abraxas   You've had very little work to do, so far. My dear chap, you don't want to go to Edinburgh now, if you can help it. Listen what comes to you on the wind –

Sounds of drunken singing of 'Danny Boy' and the smashing of glass and crockery. Fades quickly.

Mindless Dionysiac revelry, broadly typical of the Scottish character. Indeed, on morning television yesterday, a reporter on the Royal Mile yesterday couldn't find anyone sober enough to speak.

Doyle   How can you have watched morning television yesterday, if you've only arrived just now?

Abraxas   I don't know: unless I read the *Thistle*'s television review. But do keep an eye out for irregularities. If, in the intensity of my cogitation, I enter a revolving door behind you yet somehow contrive to leave in front, you should certainly raise a warning flag.

Doyle   What if Moloch arrives at Baker Street and you're not there?

Abraxas   Mr Moloch will not arrive at Baker Street to engage us tomorrow before noon. This time tomorrow we will be rolling up to his mansion set in the midst of an unpeopled wildlife experiment that was once Salisbury plain for the final encounter. Doyle, farewell.

Doyle   What happened to Winchester?

Abraxas   The very memorable last words uttered by the last bishop of Winchester, as the old bulldyke lashed herself to the falling cathedral spire. Moloch also blew up Stonehenge during a midsummer solstice rite and there was a photograph of one of the great sarsen stones, airborne from the explosion, just before it landed on the densely packed crowd. The headline read, 'Stoned Again!' That was years ago. Of course, it was immediately forgotten.

Doyle   Warning flag.

Abraxas   Let us say I read it in an old newspaper lining the cat-litter box at home.

Doyle   Holmes doesn't have a cat.

Abraxas   Right! It's not my cat, it's Schrödinger's cat which I look after for him.

Doyle   Holmes does not look after a cat for any German neighbours, either.

Abraxas   Of course you won't have seen Schrödinger's cat. It is not your average fictional cat but a quantum physics laboratory cat which I look after, whenever anti-matter matters take Herr Schrödinger away. Due to some fiendish notional experiments involving cyanide capsules triggered by random radioactive decay, it is possible to deduce, mathematically, that Schrödinger's cat, with the lid shut on its box, is both alive and dead at the same time. But Schrödinger insists I never open the box. So I never do.

Doyle   Why not?

Abraxas   If the box is opened, your sensitive little quantum particles will know they are being observed, and will behave differently, and the cat may gain another nine lives.

Doyle   Are you saying that, in science, sometimes things have to remain unobserved, to prove them satisfactory?

Abraxas   That is exactly what I am saying. Observed phenomena at the quantum level produce demonstrably different results: 'The eye altering, alters all.'

A large metal sign lights up. Illuminated from within, the letters '221B' blaze out from it. Above, a street light in the shape of a flying saucer.

This is the direction I want you to go. A few steps through that door will bring you to a room with a truckle bed containing a leaky hot-water bottle, and some off-white cotton sheets which the housekeeper hasn't changed as often as you might have wished.

Doyle   You aren't allowed to do this. We were in Scotland a moment ago.

Abraxas   I still am. I want to be alone. If anyone asks, just say Dr Watson was so drunk that he couldn't remember how he had got home that night! They'll believe you. Alcoholism runs in your family, doesn't it?

Doyle (*drunkenly*)   Not where Dr Watson lives . . . Straker Beet.

Abraxas   You can stay at Baker Street tonight. It suits me.
Off you go and try not to tipple so much in future.

*A door opens under the sign. Yellow light pours out. The door closes
and* **Doyle** *pursues the light above, as it slowly zigzags offstage.
Blackout.*

Act Two

Abraxas *is on his hands and knees. The inside of 221B Baker Street is the same minimal style as Cottingley: half an armchair with the stuffing coming out, three flying saucers going up an otherwise invisible wall.*

Abraxas   Behold the addict. I am in a hell of physical and emotional deprivation. Miserably looking for tobacco to satisfy my raw craving. With all these endless opportunities for disappointment and distress, who'd be human, eh?

Doyle   Well, you're not human, are you, Abraxas?

Abraxas   Well spotted, Dotson, Datsun, Woyle, Boyle; Eustace; whatever your name is. (*Dismissive.*) Beetle.

Pause.

Doyle   When did you arrive here?

Abraxas   Thirty-six minutes and fifty seconds ago, precisely. Almost an eternity of misery. Considering how new it must be, everything's been aged frightfully skilfully, don't you think? It may not be much, but it is home. Have you had breakfast?

Doyle   No.

Abraxas   Would you like to reconsider your plea in the light of the evidence; the recently severed parts of a kipper in the kitchen? The flesh around the fish's midriff, would you not say, bears the unmistakable stamp of a lower-middle-class underbite such as your own?

Doyle   Well, I did have a mouthful of kipper, as you recommended, but it tasted as if it had been packed in old dog-ends.

Abraxas (*shocked*)   Now I remember, I did put a kipper in a jug full of pipe dottle and old dog-ends a couple of days ago.

Doyle   But you weren't here a couple of days ago.

Abraxas   Please don't edit me before I've finished. I was trying to make up some rat-poison. Cheeky rodents were coming through the laundry chute at the back of the flat at night, chatting amongst themselves, jumping up on the sideboard and helping themselves to apples, making themselves at home. Probably using my credit cards to order fast food – (*Imitates rat, speaking on phone.*) 'A Four Seasons pizza and two milk shakes, 221B Baker Street. (*Beat.*) Just a minute! Oh my God! The cat's arrived! The invisible cat! He's eating me now. Aaah! I'm not a happy rat because I'm not a whole rat. In fact, there's only me tail left. And now even that's disappearing into the gob of Schrödinger!'

Abraxas *assumes a horrified rat-like death pose, the phone in his hand.*

Doyle   Very amusing.

Abraxas   The rats are real enough. You'll see.

Doyle   Is that prediction, or deduction?

Abraxas   To have a chance to change this black future, we may have to tinker a little with remembrance of things past. Indeed, if Baker Street is to win this battle, we must, both of us, lie not only to each other but ourselves. Sustain the mystique that you and I are a long-established enterprise, otherwise Moloch will think we're some here-today, gone-tomorrow soap bubble of fancy, which he can pop with the end of his tail. (*Pause.*) You were out for quite a while. I was worried he'd arrive before you got back.

Doyle   I was getting newspapers, as you instructed me.

Abraxas   Did you get the files from Edinburgh?

Abraxas   I got them. (*Beat.*) In a moment of temporal aphasia, I left them on the train. I'm sorry. But it doesn't matter: I pulled potted biographies of all Antipodean cosmetic surgeons off the Internet at a cybercafé at King's Cross. Not a single Queensland cosmetic surgeon in the last forty years has died in their beds. They've all had their hearts ripped out, with a pre-Inca lapis lazuli sacrificial knife. Naturally no one has ever been arrested for this unusual crime.

Doyle   I still don't see how this tail business alters the likely fate of the earth.

Abraxas   It would be clear to anyone of average intelligence. The single-minded secrecy with which Moloch has pursued his vendetta against the medical fraternity gives you some idea of how keenly he must have felt his loss. If he fails to inseminate his daughters today, his planned sacrifice of all species will be incomplete. The slaughter of Moloch's own brood, unborn, conceived on the eve of tonight's destruction through incestuous rape, is a masterstroke of evil, you must agree. But the daughters might recover from their drugged state, or Serena may hide them, and just as a master chef delays delivery of the pièce de résistance for want of a single herb that only he himself would detect, Moloch may postpone the cataclysm.

Abraxas *puts a brown bowler on* **Doyle**.

Doyle   He's not a master chef. He's a butcher. If he cannot impregnate his daughters before the cataclysm, he will still be annihilating them and their mother, as well as countless species.

Abraxas   You may have convinced yourself of that, but I know my son rather better than you. You're going to have to dumb it down a bit for when he arrives. It's not just a case of pretending to look stupid. The stupidity has to go all the way through, like the name on a stick of Brighton rock. Moloch always will find your weak spot.

Doyle   I foresee I may be hearing from you first.

Abraxas   Only because I want you to be on your guard. There's some vestigial bizarreness – erratic behaviour, recurrent in the Doyle family. Strange and rather un-

Watsonian beliefs proliferate unchallenged from theosophical circles and the Celtic fringe.

Doyle What are you getting at?

Abraxas Automatic writing, spirits . . . Don't you go in for ectoplasm and the like of an evening, regularly, with the wife and kiddies? Talking to dead people like your mother, or even more bizarrely, people who aren't there at all, and never have been? Your family circle includes a spirit counsellor called (*Sneer.*) 'Aeneas'. (*Mocking.*) 'Aeneas Speaks!'

Doyle I conduct seances with my family, my wife, and children, true. Aeneas is a kindly guiding spirit.

Abraxas 'Aeneas' actually tells you all when it would be a good time to go on holiday to Switzerland. (*Beat.*) It's a bit much to involve very young healthy children in all that hogwash, isn't it?

Doyle It's not platitudinous, to teach children that death is the gateway to further life.

Abraxas 'Aeneas' should be telling you the truth: when humans die . . . (*Snaps his fingers.*) *Rien ne va plus!* But you have bought the whole spiritualist circus. Like when Harry Houdini's mother contacted him after death. In life, as Harry told you afterwards, Mamma Houdini was an illiterate Italian peasant. She could hardly string three words of English together. (*Waves arms, mocking Italian.*) She talk-a like-a that-a! But in death, she suddenly acquired all these flowing Edwardian phrases. Oh, Doyle, please. What can I say to you? Awake, '*mia caro*', awake!

Doyle Some very eminent and responsible people are spiritualists!

Abraxas When Moloch arrives, I don't want you producing the example of young girls cutting out pictures from magazines and propping them up in the grass as being proof of anything, either. I'm not saying that you are not sincere. It's probably hereditary.

Doyle   Your meaning, sir?

Abraxas   Your father was mad enough to be put away.

Doyle   My father was periodically afflicted with a
melancholy. Not madness. I resent anyone calling it
madness.

Abraxas   But your mother did everything to keep you
from him, almost as if the taint he had was infectious.

Pause.

Doyle   Mother said it was drink. I am not sure.

Abraxas   Was it that or was it . . . general paralysis of the
insane? Was it that shape shifter, syphilis, that pushed him
out over the edge of the cliff, with nothing but air under his
feet? Even when he was dried out, hadn't touched a drop
for months, abandoned by his family, all alone in various
chilly low-priced lunatic asylum gardens, he would see little
pixies, keeking out from under geraniums – (*He imitates.*)
Squeak! Squeak! He drew them in a little book. Little folk,
for company. Day in, day out. Little twisted people who
weren't there, hatched into a half-cocked existence by rogue
spirochaetes in the spinal fluid, scratching and biting and
sometimes even nesting in his arse like the devil himself –

Doyle   I've had enough of you insulting my father!

Abraxas   You signed the form committing him! And
straight after, you went out and KILLED SHERLOCK
HOLMES!

Pause.

Doyle   For you to suggest that I do not have self-mastery,
because of some inherited disability, syphilitic or otherwise,
is hurtful, offensive and entirely unwarranted! I demand a
retraction.

Pause.

Abraxas   I retract. It was a beastly thing to suggest that your poor mad father picked up something from a working girl in the Grassmarket. He was from a highly artistic family and was probably just too frail for the harsh world of the Scottish Office of Works, poor man: enduring pawky nineteenth-century office jokes about McPixies and McGnomes all day at his desk. I'm just jealous of you having parents at all. And I'm also jealous because you are good.

Which means people love you. They also love you because you create: something memorable and engrossing, for the ride, whether it's the suburban train between Guildford and Winchester, the 'Frisco to Sausalito shuttle, the trans-Siberian express or the Tokyo bullet train . . . astronauts, lost in space, reading your bloody books. Loving them. People don't love *the creator* for what I've created. Why should they? Could there be anything worse than this, the world we are in? Can there be another, even more treacherous experience than this one, where people could be sent? No. Impossible. I have made the ultimate torment. And now to round it off, I am a character in my own private hell. Well, serves me right.

I've always lived here, alone; cigars in the coal scuttle. Bayonet – (*Mimes stab.*) – choonk! – impaling business letters to the wooden fireplace. No letters of love, personal, *billets-doux*, ever. Out-of-tune violin cats' guts, yowl, yowl. Pistol practice, bang bang, which has destroyed the rear wall. Take a look back there – the landlords would be justified in terminating the lease. I destroy the wall, Doyle, but what I really want to do after dinner sitting in my armchair is put the pistol in my mouth, and pull the trigger so my brains go splat. Then someone else with carbolic soap and a stiff brush can clear up the mystery of the great 'I am'. Not me. I'll be out of the loop. Damn you, Doyle, for creating me.

I am detestable. When I got in the cab this morning, do you know what I did? I got the cabbie to drive to Trafalgar Square, and then got on my knees with my penknife, and grubbed between the paving stones. So what do I do? Time was, the place to score was prison but not now – the prisons are all empty! Moloch knows what he's doing to make my life a misery. Well, the great man draws ever closer, devouring the wasteland in his thirty-six-point-five-ton armoured half-track, with a plume of dust pointing back across the Africanised landscape. Somewhere beyond the railhead there is a house. Serena's waiting there for Sherlock Holmes, Doyle, outside the gates of her perfectly realised prison of the mind. The chances for escape are so slim. Even if I had the key to the Ineffable, it will be useless, useless, if she doesn't recognise me.

Clock strikes.

Doyle   I'm still hazy on your hidden agenda. What exactly is the Ineffable?

Abraxas   A thing which is impossible to describe. If you do describe it, the Ineffable immediately removes its attributes from your definition, because it defies description.

Doyle   It must follow, then, that the Ineffable cannot be logically a constant, if it's always changing according to what people *say* about it.

Abraxas   True, or rather it was true, until you said it.

Doyle   I hope you're not chasing some will-o'-the-wisp, that's all.

Abraxas   You'll know I've got it right if I don't come back. (*Beat.*) Why did you take so long getting the papers?

Doyle   Just clearing a path through the hall took a while. Where did all that horse manure come from?

Abraxas   A horse's behind, unless I am mistaken. Next door, at 221A, are the offices of an animal-rights-style cab-horse sanctuary. They've been targeted by Moloch's media for an orchestrated hate-mail campaign today, their day of street demonstrations. We are getting the overflow.

Distant cries of demonstrators, whinnying of horses, and shots.

Doyle   By the time I came back, the hall had filled up again.

Abraxas   Good heavens. How long was it before your return?

Doyle   Some forty minutes, I believe.

Abraxas   Forty minutes, to pick up some newspapers from next-door downstairs?

Doyle   The time it took to walk to Euston and back.

Abraxas   But why did you go all the way to Euston, you great booby, when I had set everything up for you downstairs and you only had to ask the Patels?

Doyle   The paper shop downstairs is closed. It even says it's closed in the instruction book.

Abraxas   It never closes. It's a fact. It's down here in black and white. (*Reads.*) 'Dear Sherlock Holmes, Welcome. You can always pop down to the paper shop next door where Mr Raji Patel, who has read all your books, will greet you like an old friend. 222 Baker Street will never close –' See?

Doyle   I've read it too. Go on.

Abraxas *turns the page.*

Abraxas (*reads*)   ' . . . never close to you till the day the world ends.' (*Pause.*) I didn't realise Mr Patel was being literal. (*Beat.*) And I was looking forward to being greeted like an old friend. Patels are like beetles; innumerable, but I never met a Patel I didn't like, or take leave of without bestowing a blessing to his family. (*Beat.*) Doyle, if you found me some tobacco, I would really see you all right, you know. When the time comes. Creator's honour, for what it's worth, not much, to you, I know. Some would value it.

Doyle *produces Persian slipper.* **Abraxas** *snatches it and looks inside feverishly.*

Abraxas   Where did you find it?

Doyle   In the hall.

Abraxas *fills pipe and lights it.*

Abraxas   Bless you. Ah, the goddess Nicotine, enchantress, eternal in-dweller at the Temple of balm, whose joys may be indulged in solitude comparatively harmlessly . . . unlike my own moment of solitude, which has traduced the whole of the time-space continuum for ever.

Doyle   Well, you said it, not me.

Abraxas   I'm sorry I didn't leave you any money. You could have given yourself a hernia carrying all the Sunday papers home from King's Cross. Let's have a look, then.

Doyle *pulls a crumpled tabloid newspaper from under his jacket, slowly.*

Abraxas   Is that a complete set of Sunday papers? Surely not. Whole forests have to be felled, to satisfy one household.

Doyle   It's the *Thistle*. I didn't have any money so I had to shoplift.

Abraxas   Risky. More risky than you realise.

Doyle   No one saw me. The assistants were all watching a simulation of the future impact, on television. There's going to be a three-and-a-half-mile high tidal wave, to begin with, which travels at supersonic speed –

Abraxas   – It's not the assistants you have to worry about. God, you are a simpleton, Doyle. Have you still not worked out who we're up against? Moloch will stop at nothing to split up this team. If you leave the house now, you could be arrested – and I need you, Doyle, stuff saving this planet, I need you to get me through to the Ineffable!

Doyle (*reads from paper*)   'Our Sparky Saviour. Sergei the sparky-peckered sexpert is perched today atop a rocket and vows he will smash the meteorite. Using his miraculous electrical powers, the static star and former sex stud says he will vaporise the methane inside Caledonia so that the death-dealing meteor will explode harmlessly into a billion pieces, saving six billion human lives and unaccountable plant and animal species. Your vote, readers, will decide if Sergei is to become an overnight media superstar with his own ground-breaking cooking programme, depicting sexually explicit chargrilling.' You don't rate Sergei's chances of being launched at all?

Abraxas   It's all entertainment. If for any reason Sergei is launched, his mission is bound to fail for reasons of science. The steel mesh Moloch had the foresight to clad Caledonia with will stop any last-minute efforts at disintegration. What's this about me?

Doyle   'Sherlock Holmes arrives, centre pages.' (*Turns pages.*) 'UFO To Save World: Official. A flying saucer carrying two aliens crashed in Scotland yesterday, after losing its engine at high altitude over southern England. The aliens have survived and are undergoing tests, while a crater on Wessex Plain has been proved to contain the UFO propulsion unit after mysterious mutilations to cattle were found in the vicinity. Sherlock Holmes vows he can locate the motor which will then be used to tow the earth out of the path of the approaching juggernaut.' Entertainment, too?

Abraxas   Oh yes. Did you see any motors in the etheric pod that Moloch used as transport for his daughters? It had no motor of any kind because if it had, as soon as he had gone, the girls would have set a course for anywhere but earth. However, the UFO motor hunt will provide a motive to be beside my consort as midnight approaches. Just hope she's up for it.

Doyle   You said you didn't know how you would pull it off.

Abraxas   I'm working on it! Give the old grey matter a chance. Right, fill in our backstory. On the bookshelf in my bedroom, between Michael Jordan's *Encyclopaedia of Gods* where inexplicably, I'm not included, and the sheet music of a solo violin version of Aaron Copland's 'Fanfare for the Common Man' – there is a small but invaluable book, *Geology for All*, by R. Mutt. Learn to tell your greenstone from your shale, you needn't bother with anything which was laid down in geological time before the meteorite bombardment some sixty million years ago. The one that helped wipe out the dinosaurs. (*Pause.*) How's your back, Watson, old man? Up for a spot of digging, I hope?

Abraxas *hums, and mimes playing a violin of the Copland.*

Doyle   My back is perfectly fine, thank you, Abraxas, but my name seems to have slipped a disc. It's not Watson, except when we have company. (*Beat.*) How's *your* back, Professor?

Abraxas   Watson's the one who has to dig the hole, I'm afraid. I'm going to have my work cut out, disabusing my consort of her mundanely acquired illusions.

Resurgence of demonstration noises, then a clanking of tank treads, which stops amid screams.

Silence. **Doyle** *looks out.*

Abraxas   It's going to be Watson, from now on.

Doyle *looks out of the window;* **Abraxas** *openly snorts some coke, which* **Doyle** *observes him doing.*

Abraxas   Nothing for you to get the flag out for, Doyle. You said it was what Holmes does between jobs. (*Sniffing.*) We're not employed yet.

Doyle   Demonstrators are fleeing: either scattering or taking refuge in the cab-horse sanctuary offices.

Abraxas   I know, I know, and there will be, I expect, blood spreading over the cobbles, from under the rear tracks of a sinister-looking armoured transport.

Doyle   Are you cheating?

Abraxas   Merest deduction. On the nearside of the vehicle, there will very likely be an abandoned placard which, you can see, reads, 'Today is the day of the Horse'. Depending on which way up it has fallen, of course.

Enter **Moloch**.

Moloch   Which one of you is Sherlock Holmes?

Abraxas   I am, sir. Do you happen to have an appointment?

Moloch   I've got one with you, I suppose whether you've got one with me depends on whether you put it in your diary. You should warn visitors to arrive in gardening boots. When you had the entry hall downstairs *feng shui'd*, did they say to put the brown 'welcome' mat out fresh, every day? (*Pause.*) It's all right, I'm a good sport: I can take a joke. I've been knee-high in worse, or better; it depends on how you feel about children's blood.

Abraxas   Then you must be Mr Moloch. Good day, to you, sir. This is Doctor Foxon, I mean, Watson, my assistant.

Doyle   How do you do, sir.

Moloch   How's the quack business, then? Slow, or you wouldn't be here. (*Pause.*)

Abraxas   Congratulations on your beatitude. Is it official yet?

Moloch   I told the Vatican where they could put it. Face it, titles are for pillow-biters.

Doyle   Is there anything that I as a doctor could do about your little upset in the street just now?

Moloch   Siddown, keep your Gladstone bag shut and let
him die! I can't stand religious nuts. He was waving this
bloody placard saying 'Today is the Day of the Lord'.

Doyle   How infuriating for you. If it's anyone's day, today,
it's yours, sir. Except the placard doesn't say 'Today is the
Day of the Lord'. It says, 'Today is the Day of the *Horse*'.
Look out the window at the man you killed. The placard
reads 'Today is the Day of the *Horse*'.

Abraxas   I believe Mr Moloch has taken advantage of the
demonstration to dispose of his one remaining public
enemy, the chairperson of the Cab-horse League of Pity.

Moloch   No no, Watson's right, I can't have been looking.
I have to say, I don't mind the way it's turned out. What
these pinko shirt-lifters never credit is: if it wasn't for me,
there wouldn't be any cab-horses to get all steamed up over,
in the first place.

Abraxas   How true. Mr Moloch, have you come here
with the intention of employing us?

Moloch   I dunno about both of you. I took the liberty of
bringing up the mail.

He opens a letter with Stone-Age sacrificial knife.

An indictment for Dr Watson! Looks like you got a criminal
record, Doctor. Seen on camera shoplifting, this morning.
Charges are filed automatically, and a locum has already
taken over your practice. You're going to jail if you sit here.
If you went to the copshop now and turned yourself in,
you'd get a suspended sentence.

Hands letter to **Doyle**. **Moloch** *puts the knife away.*

Abraxas   I insist Dr Watson stays at my side today.

Moloch   Why? You should be catching people like him!

Abraxas   He's working on the Gospel of Judas for me.

Moloch   He's doing what??

Abraxas   He's translating the Gospel of Judas for me – A Gnostic fragment from the first or second century, the Gospel boasts diabolic verses suitable for keeping the spirits up in the darkest of times.

Moloch   Yeah, I know. I'd say that even more openly than the original New Testament, the Judas Gospel perversely embraces the end of all things, with joy.

Abraxas   You are familiar with this work, sir? Extraordinary. Might I ask how you came across it?

Moloch   I commissioned it. Sadly, it bombed. The sequel was sexier. Genesis, from the point of view of the snake.

Abraxas   To have been involved in publishing these highly imaginative first-century AD manuscripts, you yourself must be quite long-lived.

Moloch   I reincarnate. They were ground-breaking, for their time.

Doyle   Mr Moloch, do tell me, who did you commission the Gospel of Judas from?

Moloch   A bloke called Judas, not unnaturally. Blimey! Can you explain, Dr Watson, why you are not showing ID like the rest of the population?

Doyle   It's been a punishing schedule this last few months, toing and froing with the professor.

Moloch *picks up Persian slipper and sniffs.*

Moloch   Don't lie to me. I know Holmes only strings you along so you can get him the gear.

Doyle   I did get that for him, it's true.

Abraxas   Mr Moloch, any physician would concur with Dr Watson, that his tobacco-based treatment for my nerves is the right one. They have been badly affected by this asteroid scare.

Moloch   Come off it, you don't lie awake at night worrying about that stuff, do you? If it happens, it happens. That's all there is to it.

Abraxas   I understand from my housekeeper who watches television for me that a holy Russian is preparing to try a miracle, under your aegis.

Moloch   I'd be a fool not to bring on that story.

Abraxas   My housekeeper says the first launch opportunity passes in thirty-six and a half minutes. Since the other opportunity is close to midnight tonight and long odds, should you not be sending Sergei skywards?

Moloch   I can't launch yet. He's insisting he plays himself in the movie.

Doyle   For heaven's sake, man, what does it matter??

Abraxas   Watson, calm down. Since I understand there is no possibility of Sergei's return after this heroic mission, why not just pack him in the nose cone and reap your box-office bonanza later?

Pause.

Moloch   I could try it, I suppose.

Abraxas   Before you go – I am assuming that the task you wish to employ us for is the one already announced in today's *Thistle*.

Moloch   Yeah.

Moloch *goes to TV and turns it on.*

TV Voice (*polite Japanese accent*)   God's arsehole is about to open. Why not be like God and enjoy yourself? If you hurry you can still pamper yourself, with a luxury high-colonic irrigation –

Abraxas *turns TV off.*

Abraxas   We look forward to inspecting the marvellous new savannah I understand you've created all around your house, on the way there, and that concludes our business till then!

Moloch   As far as the wife's concerned, you're digging for bodies.

Abraxas   Mum's the word!

Moloch *exits.*

Abraxas   There is half an hour before we need to go to Waterloo to catch our train. We are going to publicise just who is the author of the coming disaster.

Doyle   It'll make no difference who knows it now!

Abraxas   You don't want people to know who killed them? I do. He's a bastard, we can't have all those people dying in ignorance of the fact. Let's splash it over the networks.

Doyle   Is this not risky?

Abraxas   It just so happens I have the perfect disguise for penetrating the Information Matrix – lobotomised, radio-controlled contract cleaners, proudly displaying the Mark of the Beast.

He hands out space-age janitor's jacket and puts one on himself, then he and **Doyle** *take on baseball hats with small yellow yo-yos on them.*

Abraxas   Beyond the rear wall there is a disused builder's chute with a minor rodent problem, which leads at a steep incline towards the heart of Moloch's London operations centre. This way.

He hands **Doyle** *a bar code which he sticks on his forehead.* **Abraxas** *follows suit.*

(*Showy.*) We now descend into the abyss! *Eins, zwei, drei!*

Blackout. Several pairs of red eyes, squeaking and twittering.

Doyle   Abraxas, something ran over my feet . . .

Abraxas   Ow! What, did you nip me, you little bastard?

Doyle   Maybe they heard about the rat poison.

Abraxas   Bit me again! Ow! I'll teach you to tie my shoelaces together!

Loud roar of falling waters; recedes. Rats depart, orderly.

Doyle   Are we there?

Abraxas   Not yet. I'm trying to remember where I've heard that fall of water before. We are far beneath things, and this is not the road to hell but somewhere close. Look away, Doyle, look away!

A flying saucer, spotlit, appears against the Richenbach falls. The saucer opens itself to reveal a red plush interior holding a round contact mine. The mine falls out and falls out of sight. Exit UFO. Water noise fades.

Abraxas   No, sorry, forget it, there is no danger in watching the Department of Plutonian Entertainment dispose of the soul of the Chairman of the Cab-horse League of Pity into the infernal Styx.

Doyle   The Styx! Are we in Hades, then?

Abraxas   No, the Styx has an outfall, outside Hades, look, where the black torrent cascades down the barren rock into Oceanus. This is the underworld's edge; yonder through the swirling mists is the bleak crag of Nevermore, where the eagle returns to nest, at night, which eats the liver of Prometheus.

The saucer enters again, and mines fall out. Exit UFO.

Doyle   Who are they burying now?

Abraxas   Oceanus is formed from tears, and sorrow will be the only reward if we press to discover beyond what should be known to mortals.

Doyle   Are you saying, you don't know?

Abraxas   If you must know, they are actually laying mines: time-delayed depth charges with a clockwork trigger which come to rest on the Fountains of the Deep.

The saucer enters again, and mines fall out. Exit UFO.

Doyle   Is the minelaying so the fountains all break up together?

Abraxas   Probably. Back into the mundane.

Effects.

Doyle   Is the Department of Plutonian Amusement involved in other aspects of the coming cataclysm?

Abraxas   They regulate ticket allocations for Planet-smashing. It is increasingly popular.

Doyle   So at midnight, who is going to be in the ringside seats?

Abraxas   Astral hoi polloi. No one important or glamorous, I imagine, retired gods, and gods whose popularity has inexplicably declined over the years. Long-term unemployed entities. Aeneas?

Effects end.

Here we are at the bottom of the disused building chute, thirty-six and a half floors below Piccadilly.

Dusty cobwebbed clothes, women's and men's, and shoes. **Abraxas** *picks up green-stained long johns.*

Doyle   Is it prudent, Abraxas, seeing the extent of this unintended detour you took us on, to try to infiltrate the Matrix now to spread the news about Moloch? You are becoming less and less reliable. Why don't we just go down to the country and you can work on your solution instead of getting lost on the way to some kind of irrelevant idealism? If people are going to die anyway, what difference does it make what they know when they die?

Abraxas Doyle, you're beginning to sound just like my son. If we manage to break into the Matrix and make a broadcast, someone could still get off the planet in time. Dammit, Doyle, this could be the way of stopping him punching mankind into oblivion!

Doyle All right. So where is the entrance?

Abraxas It has to be close. What we have here is Moloch's muniment room, with the evidence of yet more evil. Yes! A veritable treasure house if you were constructing an indictment. If you want to find out how many editors Moloch's had, just count the pairs of shoes. You saw that room we passed, full of wired bodies. Their consciousnesses are stolen and somehow put into slavery on the floor above us, the same Transformational Matrix that poor little Weegee has been taught is promotion.

Doyle Is that the only way into the Informational Matrix?

Abraxas If it is, we're stuffed.

Doyle *picks up a handbag.*

Abraxas Asthma inhaler, condoms, lipstick and thick spectacles inside the handbag of Alethea Galatea, twenty-eight years old, graduate, unmarried, member of the International Fraternity of Journalists. They last six months, if they're lucky, but you can see there's no return to the body. Alethea and all the rest end their days as electrostatic gateways for Celestial Communications Incorporated, when her imprisoned circuits burn out from sleepless finessing of the *stupor mundi*, they cease to shine and their being ceases.

Doyle Someone's coming.

Enter **Moloch** *with a bucket, meeting* **Weegee**.

Moloch Weegee. When you meet Professor Holmes take him the scenic route through the park. Show him I'm fostering any number of creatures, who without my love and attention would be extinct!

Weegee　Yes, sir. You ought to know that someone's blind drunk in the foyer. In a spacesuit.

Moloch　It's not a gutter drunk: Sergei slightly miscalculated the amount of vodka which he needed to boost his voltage, is all. Scoop him up and we'll launch him from the house tonight. (*Nods to* **Abraxas** *and* **Doyle**.) Check out these IDs.

Weegee *approaches.*

Abraxas　Evening, darlin! Retard cleaners. Wasser matter, you look like you smell a rat! (*Picks up green underwear.*) 'Ere, is this bloke ever going to put the top back on his felt-tip marker?

Weegee *goes to scan the bar codes on* **Abraxas** *and* **Doyle**, *and uses her handheld reader to consult for info.*

Weegee　There's no liaison with the disabled community in this building and there are no cleaning duties on this floor. Three six five?

Abraxas　Yeah? What of it?

Weegee　Verification ID. Should be fifteen digit. (*Of* **Doyle**.) And this one – ACD, died a hundred years ago, born . . . yesterday?

Abraxas　The Matrix may have its reasons for being a little slow tonight!

Weegee　One move, you get my stunner in your neck.

Abraxas　I was thinking – that room with the bodies: shouldn't they be woken and told it could be the end of the world? They might miss it. We could kiss the pretty ones awake . . .

Moloch　Any political affiliations?

Weegee　I've been searching. ACD has a conviction for shoplifting at 10.43 a.m. today. Three six five has convictions for failing to pay television licence, keeping an unregistered cat and for giving out false aliases.

Abraxas   I'm barking. Can't you tell?

Weegee   Barking is not listed as an alias. There is 'The Universal Self-Superannuater' –

Moloch   No – don't read them out. As long as they're not bloody horse-lovers, I don't care. Weegee – kick those clowns out.

Weegee   Sir, wait! The Matrix says it's closing itself down!

Moloch   So?

Weegee   The Matrix only closes itself down if it knows it's the end. Well, what about my promotion?

Moloch   We'll talk about it tomorrow. Meanwhile, just do your job.

Weegee *pushes* **Abraxas** *and* **Doyle** *off.*
Moloch *tosses hands et cetera, offstage, relaxed.*

Moloch (*to offstage*)   This way, girls. Come on. Come along, girls: down those steps, that's right, don't be afraid of the shadows. No one's going to hurt you.

Arsile *and* **Morgue** *arrive in tall boots, having shopped, a pair of magnificent destroying angels. They move slowly. Suggestion of red jaws and smeared lipstick.*

Arsile   What nasty beast has its lair here, so far under the earth, I wonder?

Morgue   We're lost. You said you knew the way home.

Arsile   That was before you bit the balls of that wee doorman for trying to stop us. I was totally disorientated by his screams. My ears are still ringing. What happened then?

Morgue   I can't remember either. You nipped his weasand out. That stopped him.

Moloch   Don't worry, you'll get the hang of it. You'll need to. You'll be eating for more than one.

Arsile   What are you doing here, Father?

Moloch   Waiting for you to show. Every other door was locked but this. Welcome. This is your big moment. You've come of age.

He produces two green-filled floppy plastic tubes.

Moloch   There's something I've been keeping back from you both. I'm having the etheric pod reassembled. We can leave as soon as Sherlock Holmes finds the motor. To claim your seats, you got to be good girls, and take your medicine. This is your ticket to ride. You drink this. Now all you have to do is bite the ends of these and swallow. Pretend they're lollipops.

Serena (*off*)   Wait! Arsile! Morgue!

Enter **Serena** *with machine pistol.*

Get away from him! – he's trying to kill you!

Moloch   I'm not forcing them to do anything they don't want. (*To* **Arsile** *and* **Morgue**.) I've laid on a feast here. I know hunting takes time, and we don't have much of it. If you fancy a bite, there's plenty. Chilled or fresh.

Arsile   Forget it.

Moloch   The girls know what the score is. It's not what you think.

Serena   So what is going on?

Arsile   It's a long story, and you don't know most of it. Briefly, he's our father and he wants to breed from us.

Serena   Just say no!

Morgue   We would anyway. It's our way. Then father would put three foot of barbed tail up your jacksie, with no by-your-leave.

Moloch That's not happening now, is it? Am *I* threatening anyone? Arsile and Morgue, you need to consider the big picture. Pass on your chance now, I remind you that you will revert into being short-term dumb meat harvesters. And there's only eight hours to go till the food chain here goes down. If you don't want to take advantage of this noble opportunity for your species, get out of here and take your chances.

Serena While I'm still alive, I'm going to be seeing no harm comes to those girls.

Moloch Not girls for long. A musculo-skeletal shift is occurring, which means soon they'll be able to do clever stuff like dig out worms from their arses with their tongues. Not that they'll live long enough to get raw meat parasites. Get ready to shoot 'em full of tranquillisers; they've got twice the number of teeth they had at four o'clock. By the time they get home, they'll have lost the power of speech. They won't be remotely grateful to you for sticking up for them, in fact they won't recognise you: by midnight, they'll happily tear you apart!

Serena I will accept whatever is in your nature, but I reject the monstrousness that is yours. I should have known you were inhuman. This way, girls.

Exit **Serena**, *guarding* **Arsile** *and* **Morgue**.

Blackout. Whistle of train. Elephants trumpet. Lights.

Announcer 'Melchester Parkway, Melchester Parkway. We apologise for the late arrival of the last train from Waterloo; this was due to a genetically modified rhinoceros which charged the locomotive and burst the boiler.'

Weegee *now has a tail, made of plaited electric leads, going down to the floor. She leads* **Doyle** *and* **Abraxas**.

Weegee This way, Professor, and Dr Watson. Dear oh dear, you are late. The sun's going down fast.

Abraxas *and* **Doyle** *get into a tall hackney, with* **Moloch** *crest on the side.* **Weegee** *mounts the driving seat and drives off. Horses clopping hooves.* **Doyle** *and* **Abraxas**, *facing each other.*

Abraxas   I've been thinking. It does not matter we left before the end, I know Serena's character well enough. She will simply not have allowed him to get to the girls.

Doyle   So?

Abraxas   So, a great deal.

Weegee   Mr Moloch wanted you to note those mighty-trunked trees along the way, grey giants, their bark thick-scarred? He wants you to know, seven Zeppelins were lost, ferrying baobabs from Madagascar. Those hairy elephants tusking the bark for forage are unique mastodons, back bred from sperm found in Alaskan glaciers, likewise the fearsome sabre-toothed tiger, whose lair we are about to pass. These nocturnal predators proved such efficient killers they almost upset the delicate ecological balance that Mr Moloch had established. The tiger's kill rate reduced to controllable levels after genetic manipulation of their genes made them fluorescent, and advertised their night-time presence to the buffalo.

Doyle   'Tiger, tiger, burning bright,
   In the forests of the night;
   What immortal hand or eye,
   Could frame thy fearful symmetry!'

Weegee   What did you say, sir?

Doyle   It wasn't me speaking – William Blake.

Abraxas (*a great cry*)   I've got it. It's been given to me on a plate! The twins, defying their father is the final breakthrough, Doyle! Now all the conditions can be satisfied. 'The body of the Logos must pass through twin virgins who have themselves turned against the dark seed of the Word.' Moloch's two daughters – twin virgins – have turned against him. Moloch being the dark seed of the Word. Me being the Logos.

Doyle   How does the Logos propose to 'pass through' the twin virgins, and still keep their virginity?

Abraxas   Easy. They eat me.

Doyle   So have I been wasting my time reading up R. Mutt?

Abraxas   Not at all.

Bellowing of hippos.

Weegee   Hippopotamus over there, in a swamp under Mr Moloch's protection.

Abraxas   Thank you, Weegee! What splendid creatures they are to be sure. If they could speak, I'm sure their first sentence would acclaim your master as their natural monarch.

Weegee   I've been thinking, that if this really is the end, it's just sad all these species are going to die as well as us. Do you think they really don't know?

Abraxas   What animals know and don't know is problematic. But one would like to think they know the truth.

Weegee   I just realised this is the end. I don't know why it's taken so long. This really is the end! I don't have a future.

Abraxas   It's never really the end. The odd cockroach and diatom always pull through; besides, mother nature is always pelting this lucky planet with snowballs full of all kinds of interesting life forms.

Weegee   Thank you, I have a perfectly interesting life form right here.

Abraxas   Nature is prodigal. Seven whole distinct phenotypes were found in the Burgess Shale. There are only twelve now on the planet. The seven are all extinct now, of course.

Weegee　Any significance in the number seven?

Abraxas　None, in this case, unfortunately.

Doyle　I need the names of the Seven *now*. Abraxas, you heard me.

Abraxas　I could be penalised, for giving them out too soon. Only four Immortals need to take that decision. And I tell you, at least four don't like me.

Weegee　Pardon me for overhearing. Why are there Seven Immortals?

Abraxas　There used to be twelve, but they fell out over the function of Beauty. (*Horse farts. Beat.*) Correction from my learned friend there. Gas; chaos! It wasn't *beauty* on its own the Twelve fell out about, it was how beauty stood in relation to *chaos*, the prime matter.

Doyle　How does beauty relate to chaos?

Abraxas　Poorly. (*Horse farts again.*) – Or not at all, as my learned friend suggests. Five Immortals resigned, saying this universe had been created on a false premise, the first lie, if you like, which would lead it to be dominated by evil and destruction, with badly designed creatures roaming round constructed largely out of the rubble of former collisions. Monsters. And they were right. Look at you. Everything is tainted. The traces of gold in your blood was forged in the clumsy unintentional death throes of stars. Man is the receptacle, resonating with everything that has happened; sadly, the original material is fatally flawed. Meanwhile for me, from now on, it's goodbye, cruel colliding worlds. Goodbye, bad biology. Goodbye, cut-and-shut universe.

Clip-clops stop. **Weegee** *whips the horse.*

Weegee　Get a move on then, you brainless piece of meat.

Weegee *lashes at the horse, and curses it in Chinese.*

Abraxas   No, no. Don't say Dobbin's stupid, Weegee. The smell of death is in the air, and this sapient beast sees his own end foreshadowed in a fellow ruminant's demise. Look away from the road a little, and tell me what you see.

Weegee *shines torch into darkness.*

Weegee   Oh wow. I don't known if I'm up to a description.

Doyle   The body of a Thomson's gazelle. With some very curious mutilations. Something has cut the lips and eyes out . . . almost surgically . . . and at the other end, it's as if the anus has been precisely cored. (*Clip-clops resume.*)

Abraxas   So what do you think caused that, Weegee?

Weegee   It's not lions, who stifle the prey by putting the animal's head in their mouths. It could conceivably be jackals, which generally go into the body through the soft tissues round the back passage. But you'd surely hear the pack barking. I've not seen anything like it outside alien contact websites on the Net.

Abraxas   Quite so, Weegee, when the impossible has been excluded, the improbable becomes the only answer. Dr Watson, which creature have we encountered recently that nipped out a windpipe and testicles with surgical precision, but is new to the novel hierarchy of Moloch's savannah? *Gaudeamus igutur! Puellae Molochii adveniunt!*

Weegee   I'm sorry, sir. You might have Mandarin, but I don't have Latin.

Abraxas   'Rejoice, for the girls have arrived here before us.' Twin virgins, who themselves have turned against the Dark Seed of the Word.

Doyle (*flash of light*)   Oh my giddy aunt!

Abraxas   Nothing to worry about, yet. That was no bigger than a peanut. When Caledonia breeches, you'll feel it through the soles of your feet.

A floodlit (model) house, somewhat like the White House, pillared and porticoed, covered in satellite dishes, revealed upstage. A sign hand-painted, 'CHILD MURDER INVESTIGATION AREA', in foreground, which spins to reveal another sign, 'UFO INVESTIGATION AREA'.

Clip-clops stop. A full moon, behind the house.

Weegee   This is where Mr Moloch wants you to start. I've got to go polish his tail harness.

Doyle   Your master has a tail?

Weegee   Oh yeah.

Abraxas   You look like you're growing one yourself.

Weegee   These were subdermal implant leads for my electronic profile, but it looks like tomorrow's cancelled. Hey, I'm going nowhere so I'm making an ironic statement.

Abraxas   You must know now quite a lot about Mr Moloch's connections with Caledonia.

Weegee   I had my suspicions, sure.

Abraxas   You're going to work for him to the end, then?

Weegee   It's too late to rebel. Some time ago, I realise now, he ate my soul. Might as well keep busy.

She exits.

Doyle   She mentioned a tail harness. You said Moloch's tail was lost at birth.

Abraxas   I can't see how the issue is going to affect anything now. The girls are beyond taming, defiant.

Doyle   I don't think you should wait to give me the names.

Abraxas   There's thirty-six-point-five seconds between the first seismic shock, and the arrival of the supersonic three-mile-high tidal wave of dilute nitric acid. In that time I could give you the names of dozens of Immortals.

Doyle   I don't like this arrangement. You have made too many significant mistakes. Do you even know all Seven names, Abraxas?

Abraxas   What! The puny mortal challenges the Archon's access to the Akashic record? I shall overlook your insolence and begin the awakening of my better half. If you want to help me, do not let Moloch suspect for a moment that we keep any other agenda than the one he has set. Dig deep, and loud while I work on Serena, and in God's good time, you will be rewarded for your labour. The Logos gives you his word. Nothing is more binding than that.

Enter **Serena**, *holding machine pistol.* **Doyle** *digs.* **Abraxas** *goes to* **Serena**.

Abraxas   Good evening, madam.

Serena   So, Professor Holmes, my husband has kept his word for once. Inexplicable, but no doubt you can tell me exactly what is going on.

Abraxas   A man I shall call 'Dr Watson' and myself are supposed to be investigating long-buried crimes, for your so-called husband, while simultaneously pretending to perform another entirely bogus investigation. All of the above is appearance and can be discarded. Since time is so short, I should make the underlying theme plain to you as rapidly as possible. It is that you and I are one.

Serena   I don't care how you count us, if I die tonight, I want to see these bones.

Abraxas   You can't see them if they are not there. The truth is, this can be our moment of breakthrough, Serena. If you can trust me, you and I will be able to escape to the Ineffable, together.

Serena   Are you suggesting I leave my husband?

Abraxas   Your apparent husband, as I said, yes, for me.

Serena   Dr Watson declared us married yesterday. I didn't realise he was actually pandering for you.

Abraxas   Dr Watson is no procurer. He and I see eye to eye on almost everything except fairies. You have been deluded by a venom, and now you can awake. And together we must pass through the portals to the Ineffable together before midnight if at all.

Serena   I thought Sherlock Holmes was going to be my saviour, but you make no sense at all.

Abraxas   Quickly then. You have a memory of twenty years ago, your so-called husband savagely killing your children here?

Serena   Yes I do. Exactly here, upon this spot.

Abraxas   This distance from the house, do you think you saw Moloch standing here baying the moon, with your children's limp headless bodies about his feet, a little broken skull in each hand, his chin dribbling brains and blood?

Serena   Those are the exact pictures in my mind. How did you know, Professor Holmes?

Abraxas   Call me Abraxas. The remains, he buried on this spot, did he not? – Moloch using his forearms with prodigious skill and speed, to dig a hole?

Serena   Just so. It was terrible, terrible.

Abraxas   It was terrible, and untrue. There are no human children buried here. In fact, you had no children with him. You never married him. You first set eyes upon him yesterday when you arrived with me.

Enter **Moloch** *who stares into the hole.*

Serena   Surely we were married?

Moloch   Of course we were. A thousand choirboys were castrated to sing for our wedding. Asphodels a foot thick, strewn for miles round the wedding feast –

Serena   Yes, yes.

Moloch   I wish someone would tranquillise those aliens, Serena. If we survive tonight there's going to be practically nothing left alive in the park. They are proving bloody insatiable. (*Beat.*) Found anything yet?

Doyle   Not yet.

Moloch   Keep up the good work, Watson.

Abraxas   What happened to Sergei?

Moloch   Put it this way, we're more than ever dependent on Watson, now.

Serena   It was actually a human sacrifice. This good old man, glowing gently, was led out and put in the place of the warhead of an ancient rocket which caught fire, and burnt up like a roman candle, without taking off from the lawn. My husband's expression watching it was pure delight.

Moloch   I was taking inspiration from the Gospel of Judas. That won't mean anything to you, dear. It's a way of meeting the worst with a smile!

Exits.

Abraxas   Does the name Abraxas still mean nothing to you, madam? I am Abraxas, your beloved. Abraxas. Believe that and let all else melt away. Accept that you have been my consort, for eternity.

Serena   Bride to Abraxas! The idea is strangely attractive. Give me time.

Abraxas   We don't have time. The truth is, Serena, that you and I are Pan's godparents, ancient overlords, the Old Ones. However, all is flux; old gods pass away. To step through to the Ineffable together, we need to place ourselves on the menu of Moloch's daughters.

Serena   What would you have them do?

Abraxas   Oblige us here. Simply eat me, first, then you. Those are the terms for release. Can you call them?

Serena   I can try but they are very wild now. When we got back I opened the ballroom windows and played the piano till my fingers almost bled: they would not approach. (*Calls.*) Kitty-kitty-kitty-kitty!

Enter **Moloch**.

Abraxas   Dr Watson! Anything to report, down there, to Mr Moloch?

Doyle *pops up his head out of the hole.*

Doyle   I've worked my way down to the bottom of a comparatively fresh soil chimney. The gravel moraine I'm now going through, I would say, is relatively undisturbed so rather less promising. It contains fragments of knapped flints from the earliest settlers who moved on to this then-fertile territory after the collapse of the last ice age, perhaps ten thousand years ago.

Moloch   That's laid out Serena's hopes for justice, cold. She was hoping you were going to find a nest of freshly crushed babies' skulls.

Exit **Moloch**.

Abraxas   Don't stop, Doyle. Deeper, ever deeper.

Doyle *throws up the soil industriously.*

Doyle   Here's something. Mixed in with the earliest flints are fragments of pottery from the Beaker folk, a sophisticated civilisation. There is certainly continuing evidence for humanity to between fifty and a hundred thousand years ago. But then it ceases. I'm now passing two million years ago, and any relics left, hand tools and so on, are getting pretty scarce.

Serena   Agh! I have started to remember things now. You are indeed my beloved and I see we will be free if we follow your plan, to go to the highest realm possible.

Abraxas   Excellent. But tickle up our brokers, quickly now. Allow them to approach me first, then you follow.

Serena   Are you sure this is going to work?

Abraxas   Oh, there's no pain on the path to the Ineffable. I understand it is as if the doors open to the finest vintage of un-being, and you depart.

Serena   Very well. I commit. (*Calls.*) Kitty-kitty-kitty-kitty!

Doyle   I am now going through layers of Cretaceous and Jurassic deposits and Lower Old Red sandstone. I would say nothing has disturbed these deposits for twenty, thirty million years. And now there's a curious uniform dark discoloration band, between the strata. This could be the one deposited after the last meteor strike; the one which annihilated the dinosaurs sixty million years ago. Yes! A band of rare iridium salts, evidence for the earth's periodic reforging, in the foundry of the stars! Abraxas – if I'm not mistaken, the iridium layer is starting to glow –?!

Lighting effects from the hole.

Abraxas   Nothing unusual. Molecular memory; universal sympathy and so forth.

Enter **Arsile** *and* **Morgue** *on all fours. They halt.*

Serena   Something is stopping them.

Abraxas   Put the gun away.

Serena *puts the gun down.* **Arsile** *and* **Morgue** *approach and start to consume* **Abraxas**.

Abraxas   That's better. Doyle, Serena and I are at long last going through. Thank you for covering for us. Bounteous Spirit, Good Mind, Truth and Right-mindedness, are the Seven names.

Doyle   That's only four.

Morgue *eats* **Serena** *who shrieks.*

Abraxas   Just a slight twinge surely. It's most delightful.

Serena   I'll try and be brave.

Doyle   That's only four names you've given me. Serena – are you familiar with the Seven Immortals?

Serena   No, and I've always been terrible with names, I'm afraid.

Doyle   Abraxas! I need three more names!

Abraxas   You need what? No panic, we'll do it another way. There are more ways to kill a cat than . . . See the Zodiac up there? There's a handy little mnemonic built into the circle of animals. (*Beat.*) I've forgotten it. Shakespeare's got the answer as usual. 'In me thou see'st the twilight of such day, as after sunset fadest in the West; which by and by black night doth take away, Death's second self, that seals up all in rest.' . . . Hot booty! I'm shooting the rapids of molten tin on Mercury, in a burning canoe!

Doyle   Three names, Abraxas!

Abraxas   There's ullage in life's wine, as well as lees. Come close. (**Doyle** *approaches.*) Doyle, humanity is a spreading poison. Scum. Give yourself away to the girls quickly. Let them start on your toes and work up. Don't go back to your earth. Forget the wife and kids. Come with us. It is a most thrilling transgression. Schrödinger. Schrödinger.

Doyle   I don't think any of the Seven Immortals are called after a twentieth-century quantum physicist!

Abraxas   Come on, pusscat. Going, going, gone.

Glugging noises, disappears. **Serena** *disappears.*

Serena   I come, Abraxas!

Doyle   Speak to me! I charge you, Ur-Archon Abraxas Three Six Five, tell me THE NAMES!

Serena *and* **Abraxas** *are eaten. Enter* **Moloch***, dressed in great pomp, with black crown, long tail.* **Arsile** *and* **Morgue** *flee.*

Moloch Serena warned you, did she not, against invoking his full name or the fountains of the deep break up. And they are about to break up, and it's all your fault! Better believe me, for I the despis-éd son of Abraxas am now taking up my rightful inheritance. Bow down and worship me, and take every word I utter as gospel. On your knees, if you please. (**Doyle** *assumes boxing mode.*) That is not a worship mode I recognise. Are you trying to pick a fight now? Why?

Doyle Because I have witnessed you in the last two days, grievously deluding and mentally tormenting a lady. (**Moloch** *laughs.*) The fact is you are a universal infernal pest. (**Moloch** *laughs.*) Indeed there is no deadly sin which your character does not willingly embrace, so up with your dukes, man!

Doyle *tries to punch him and* **Moloch** *waves the punch aside.*

Moloch You pathetic little pipsqueak. Don't even think about it. I always win! No Queensberry rules, here. No duality of good and evil, falling down the Richenbach Falls in a slow fade. If I were you, I would do your best not to offend the new governor, or he could rip your heart out. Now quiet down while I take stock. Something needs my attention in the new bailiwick.

Music, Russian Orthodox Mass. A round, glowing crystal rises out of the hole, magically.

Moloch There it is. Oh dear. Sergei the holy Russian is under the impression he's entering Orthodox heaven. We can't have that.

Orthodox Mass abruptly ceases, with the scratching sound of a knocked stylus. The light of the crystal dies.

Doyle Why did you pretend your tail had been lost?

Moloch Arsile and Morgue had to plausibly stay virgins, if the old bugger was to work out how to take a dive.

Doyle I think this needs looking into. Why pretend a disablement which would in fact allow your enemy to gain the Ineffable?

Moloch Good question! No spots on Dr Watson! The bottom line. When the Dayspring from on high passes over, the Dark one inherits everything, including that which is not formed, and inchoate. The contract says, I get control of the Ineffable. And Abraxas is going to be where he belongs, under my thumb. And for everyone including those in the Ineffable, it's the tourist-class Infernal Shades from now on: Move it! One shade fits all! As for you, little man, I'd go home and enjoy yourself, while you can.

Doyle I would but Abraxas left me three names short.

Moloch Typical. I'll let you go if you tell the world how the old bastard dropped you in it, and how it was his much misunderstood offspring set you free. I'll even throw you in three wishes. No kidding. Straight offer. Nothing up my sleeve.

Doyle I think anyone should be careful of what they ask for, from you. (*Beat.*) I want Sergei to enter Orthodox heaven.

Moloch A bloke you don't even know? Blimey! That's needlessly generous. All right. One wish.

Russian Mass starts again. The crystal lights.

Doyle My second wish is that Abraxas and Serena are to be released to the Ineffable. Thirdly, a message to my mother –

Moloch That's your lot! Abraxas and Serena each count as one. That's three wishes and your lot. So no mothers. I got an errand for you. I'm sick of the sledging I've been getting. I want to see articles saying I'm likeable. Tell 'em I

set you free. 'Hats off to Dark Lord!' 'Evil Incarnate turns
Rescuer.' 'Famous Author's Gratitude.'

Doyle   Mr Moloch, stop. A reputation for integrity, once
lost, is hard to regain. If you wish someone to fashion prose
for you after a designated headline, an independent author
is hardly your man.

Moloch   I just gave you three wishes! Want me to take
'em back?

Doyle   If you want praise on earth go there and set your
system up. We are not yet so slavishly automated yet.

Moloch   Semi-automated. I almost got rid of journos.
Well, it doesn't sound as if I'm going to be able to call in any
favours from you, does it? All right, bugger off home. Let's
see, the names you need are (*Pause.*) Dominion, Health, and
oh dear! The last fellow's name has been inexplicably erased
from the Akashic Record! It says, 'Refer to Ineffable.' We all
know who's in there. And it's electrodes on the genitals,
there is no other way, to jog Abraxas' memory.

Doyle   Leave him in peace, you great sadistic bully!

Moloch   All right, I'll leave him in the Ineffable, but you'll
never guess the last name.

Doyle   Oh no? (*Pause.*) It's Life, isn't it? The name of the
seventh Immortal. Life. (*Pause.*)

Moloch   Mmm. Maybe Watson's not stupid after all.
Maybe he is. Time will tell. Not long to go. Tick, tick,
tick . . .

Doyle   The deduction is hardly taxing to explain even in
the short time left. It is your character, sir, which betrays
you. Life is everything which all your diabolical ingenuity
has been aimed to pervert, twist, and negate on the altar of
your vile self. Anyone familiar with the Mesopotamian
influence in Judaism would have come to the same
conclusion as I have.

Moloch   Oh, I'm sure the old chum Abraham left clues for you pinned up all over the sheep-dip. Naa! Seven's not a wild card, this hand. You got a busted flush. (*Beat.*)

Doyle   On the contrary. The seven candles on the menorah stand for the seven visible heavenly bodies which are the Seven Immortals in another guise. You only think you hold the aces in this game, sir. The name of the greatest Immortal is handed down in the toast that the Jews raise their glasses to! *L'chaim!* To Life!

Moloch   A charming notion, Doyle. But no use to man, or beast.

Doyle   We'll see.

Moloch *exits.*

A clock on the house starts to chime like a tinny Big Ben. Light starts to flicker faster and faster. Lighting change to ghastly grey-green. A great awesome thump as Caledonia strikes. Stage flooded with red light. Rumbling, and Moloch Hall collapses. The front pillars roll around. Stage floods with smoke. Approaching roar of the tidal wave. The moon turns blood red.

Doyle (*confident*)   Bounteous Spirit! Good Mind! Truth! Right-mindedness! Dominion, Health! LIFE!

Smoke slowly clears. Sound slowly dies. **Doyle** *on his knees. Moon in same place but now a pale afternoon moon. Below the moon the Cottingley glade resumes. Enter* **Weegee** *dressed Edwardian again, as in beginning. She goes and helps Doyle up, and dusts him down.*

Weegee   What's going on, sir? I heard these cries. I thought you might be having a heart attack. Well, it is more likely than seeing goblins, particularly at your age? (*Beat.*)

Doyle   Miss Undine . . . Does the Old Testament god Moloch, mean anything to you?

Weegee   No. What did he do?

Doyle   I don't know what he did. It just says the children of the Israelites were made holocaust, that is, sacrificed in an ordeal by fire to him. I also wanted to check . . . Do you happen to know where a petrol station is?

Weegee Didn't we just fill up just before we got to Cottingley?

Doyle Of course. I forgot.

Weegee I'll finish packing the car.

Doyle Thank you, Miss Undine.

Exit **Weegee**. **Doyle** *turns to audience.*

And that was the end of the Cottingley haunting. No fairies were found on the negatives, true. But I leave the sceptics among us – and there must be some – with this question. Who has overseen the living apothecary of nature, since ancient times, on our behalf, if not entities? How, ladies and gentlemen, in one small space could there be a cornucopia of plants as in Cottingley, plants useful to man, unless there are active guardians, identified with our welfare who are looking after these wild plants for us, until we are wise enough to reap the benefits? In one corner of this enchanted wood alone, I saw marigold, a saffron substitute, as well as medicinal eyebright; fat hen, that guardian against the scurvy; foxgloves in profusion – which yield digitalis, for unsteady hearts; and a clump of what the Welsh, I think, call bears' garlic, from the hellebore family anyway, very useful against all kinds of mental confusion . . .

Rest of cast joins him. Music, reprise.

A SELECTED LIST OF
METHUEN MODERN PLAYS

☐ CLOSER	Patrick Marber	£6.99
☐ THE BEAUTY QUEEN OF LEENANE	Martin McDonagh	£6.99
☐ A SKULL IN CONNEMARA	Martin McDonagh	£6.99
☐ THE LONESOME WEST	Martin McDonagh	£6.99
☐ THE CRIPPLE OF INISHMAAN	Martin McDonagh	£6.99
☐ THE STEWARD OF CHRISTENDOM	Sebastian Barry	£6.99
☐ SHOPPING AND F***ING	Mark Ravenhill	£6.99
☐ FAUST (FAUST IS DEAD)	Mark Ravenhill	£5.99
☐ COPENHAGEN	Michael Frayn	£6.99
☐ POLYGRAPH	Robert Lepage and Marie Brassard	£6.99
☐ BEAUTIFUL THING	Jonathan Harvey	£6.99
☐ MEMORY OF WATER & FIVE KINDS OF SILENCE	Shelagh Stephenson	£7.99
☐ WISHBONES	Lucinda Coxon	£6.99
☐ BONDAGERS & THE STRAW CHAIR	Sue Glover	£9.99
☐ SOME VOICES & PALE HORSE	Joe Penhall	£7.99
☐ KNIVES IN HENS	David Harrower	£6.99
☐ BOYS' LIFE & SEARCH AND DESTROY	Howard Korder	£8.99
☐ THE LIGHTS	Howard Korder	£6.99
☐ SERVING IT UP & A WEEK WITH TONY	David Eldridge	£8.99
☐ INSIDE TRADING	Malcolm Bradbury	£6.99
☐ MASTERCLASS	Terrence McNally	£5.99
☐ EUROPE & THE ARCHITECT	David Grieg	£7.99
☐ BLUE MURDER	Peter Nichols	£6.99
☐ BLASTED & PHAEDRA'S LOVE	Sarah Kane	£7.99

• All Methuen Drama books are available through mail order or from your local bookshop.

Please send cheque/eurocheque/postal order (sterling only) Access, Visa, Mastercard, Diners Card, Switch or Amex.

☐☐☐☐☐☐☐☐☐☐☐☐☐☐☐☐

Expiry Date: _____ Signature: _____

Please allow 75 pence per book for post and packing U.K.
Overseas customers please allow £1.00 per copy for post and packing.

ALL ORDERS TO:

Methuen Books, Books by Post, TBS Limited, The Book Service, Colchester Road, Frating Green, Colchester, Essex CO7 7DW.

NAME: _____

ADDRESS: _____

_____

_____

Please allow 28 days for delivery. Please tick box if you do not wish to receive any additional information ☐

Prices and availability subject to change without notice.

Methuen Contemporary Dramatists
include

Peter Barnes (three volumes)
Sebastian Barry
Edward Bond (six volumes)
Howard Brenton
  (two volumes)
Richard Cameron
Jim Cartwright
Caryl Churchill (two volumes)
Sarah Daniels (two volumes)
Nick Darke
David Edgar (three volumes)
Ben Elton
Dario Fo (two volumes)
Michael Frayn (two volumes)
Paul Godfrey
John Guare
Peter Handke
Jonathan Harvey
Declan Hughes
Terry Johnson (two volumes)
Bernard-Marie Koltès
David Lan
Bryony Lavery
Doug Lucie
David Mamet (three volumes)

Martin McDonagh
Duncan McLean
Anthony Minghella
  (two volumes)
Tom Murphy (four volumes)
Phyllis Nagy
Anthony Nielsen
Philip Osment
Louise Page
Joe Penhall
Stephen Poliakoff
  (three volumes)
Christina Reid
Philip Ridley
Willy Russell
Ntozake Shange
Sam Shepard (two volumes)
Wole Soyinka (two volumes)
David Storey (three volumes)
Sue Townsend
Michel Vinaver (two volumes)
Michael Wilcox
David Wood (two volumes)
Victoria Wood